A
Taxonomy
of the
Psychomotor Domain

A Taxonomy of the Psychomotor Domain

A Guide for Developing Behavioral Objectives

Anita J. Harrow

DAVID McKAY COMPANY, INC. • NEW YORK

To my husband, Thomas

Preface

This text has as its broad concern the provision of a model which can be utilized by educators to assist them in becoming more efficient in organizing their instructional goals and to better evaluate achievement of learning concerned with cognitive, affective, and psychomotor behaviors. The specific intent of this text is to provide a functional written taxonomy for the psychomotor domain to be utilized for the classification of observable movement behaviors. The classification levels within the model are hierarchically arranged along a continuum from the lowest level of psychomotor behavior to the highest level. This taxonomy will make it possible for educators to identify and classify behaviors unique to the psychomotor domain. It will act as a guide for educators concerned with preparing a meaningful sequential curriculum utilizing appropriate instructional strategies, and selecting relevant measurement techniques. Working with this type of a framework, educators will be able to make possible more meaningful experiences focused upon improved psychomotor development of children.

The following strategies were utilized to develop this model for classifying movement behaviors of children. The movement literature was thoroughly reviewed. The categorizations of movement components advocated by various authors were studied and compared to ascertain similarities which might prove beneficial to the evolving taxonomy. Pertinent definitions were collected, compared, selected and modified where necessary to provide a common base upon which to develop this functional model.

Theories of child growth and development were studied and compared since the taxonomy was to have a developmental foundation. Select educators were requested to review the taxonomy to verify the communicability of the model. Current research and on-going programs were also reviewed in an effort to select and organize stated educational objectives to serve as a guide for sophistication of the classification levels within the taxonomy.

The author wishes to express sincere gratitude and appreciation to the individuals who have assisted in some way in the development of this text.

Special acknowledgement and sincere gratitude are extended to Dr. Mary F. Hall who stimulated the author's first thoughts about developing a taxonomy for the psychomotor domain, to Dr. Etta Walters who provided guidance and helpful suggestions for relevant background readings, and to Dr. Kenneth Miller for his valuable assistance in reviewing the manuscript.

To Dr. H. H. McAshan, the author is deeply indebted for his encouragement, interest, and helpful criticisms of the manuscript.

Anita J. Harrow
August, 1971

Contents

List of Figures

CHAPTER I

Introduction and Explanation of the Psychomotor Domain

This model proposed for classifying movement behaviors unique to the psychomotor domain has been designed specifically to aid educators and curriculum developers to clarify and categorize relevant movement experiences for children. It has six classification levels with corresponding subcategories, and where necessary these subcategories are further analyzed into divisions.

The basic structure of the taxonomic model that follows is offered as a way of viewing, explaining, and categorizing learner's movement behaviors.

1.00 Reflex Movements
    1.10 Segmental Reflexes
    1.20 Intersegmental Reflexes
    1.30 Suprasegmental Reflexes
2.00 Basic-Fundamental Movements
    2.10 Locomotor Movements
    2.20 Non-Locomotor Movements
    2.30 Manipulative Movements
3.00 Perceptual Abilities
    3.10 Kinesthetic Discrimination
    3.20 Visual Discrimination
    3.30 Auditory Discrimination
    3.40 Tactile Discrimination

3.50   Coordinated Abilities
4.00   Physical Abilities
     4.10   Endurance
     4.20   Strength
     4.30   Flexibility
     4.40   Agility
5.00   Skilled Movements
     5.10   Simple Adaptive Skill
     5.20   Compound Adaptive Skill
     5.30   Complex Adaptive Skill
6.00   Non-Discursive Communication
     6.10   Expressive Movement
     6.20   Interpretive Movement

The following chapters are composed of background information, a review of the rationale for developing a taxonomy for the psychomotor domain, and a discussion of problems inherent in classifying behaviors unique to this particular domain. Various explanations regarding movement categories and explanations of previously developed schemas for the classification of educational objectives in the psychomotor domain will be explored.

Following the information section is the detailed explanation of the classification levels, the subcategories and, where applicable, the divisions of this model for classifying movement behaviors. Once the reader has a familiarity with the entire model, he is ready to begin classifying movement behaviors.

The next section of this text provides an illustration of how the model could be utilized for developing behavioral objectives. Numerous examples of behavioral objectives are provided. Many of them could be taken without modification and included as part of a behaviorally stated curriculum. However, it is recommended that the reader treat the examples provided as guides and develop a behaviorally stated curriculum to meet the identified psychomotor needs of his particular group of children. All of the behavioral objective examples used in this text are developed by the goals approach.

The last section of this text concerns itself with the relevant literature and essential terminology. This actually represents the basis for the development of this taxonomy for the psychomotor domain.

Throughout the entire book, McAshan's[1] goals approach for writing behavioral objectives has been utilized. By using this writing technique, the educational goal or learning task is explicitly stated, which makes selection of a relevant measurement of the goal easier to accomplish. Using this writing approach also facilitates the organization of curriculum content in behavioral terms and communicates the objectives more precisely than do other writing approaches. This technique also fulfills the educator's concern for accountability in that if his curriculum is stated in behavioral terms utilizing this particular writing technique, he has his educational intentions outlined and the relevancy of pupils' performances is more obvious.

IMPORTANCE OF PSYCHOMOTOR BEHAVIORS

The major activities of primitive man revolved around the development of physical efficiency, group

---

[1] H. H. McAshan, *Writing Behavioral Objectives: A New Approach* (New York: Harper & Row, 1970).

membership, and recreation. A test of early man's physical efficiency was his ability to meet the challenge of survival. He depended on his physical prowess to meet the rigors of daily life and to compete with his natural environment. Not only did his individual survival depend upon his physical attributes of agility, strength, and speed, but also the survival of the group was dependent upon the physical efficiency of its members.

In early societies the basic activities included hunting, fishing, and food gathering. Man's leisure included activities requiring low organization, activities involving dexterity and skill, and activities of childhood drama in anticipation of later adult roles. Creative movement, or dancing, was essential in the life of early man serving both a religious-magic and a festive function.

The physical and mental education of primitive man consisted of both formal and informal activities. Informal education, which covered the physical and practical activities of life, encompassed a major portion of this education. In primitive society, the psychomotor objectives were obvious to everyone and their satisfactory development was essential for the continued existence of the tribe. The struggle for life in those days demanded that man remain active in a directly useful manner.

People participate in a variety of activities today for a number of reasons, including recreation, health, the intrinsic pleasures derived from movement, and economic gain as professional performers. The bases for the sportive activity of primitive man originated with his natural desire for movement and his religious beliefs and practices, in addition to his utilitarian pursuits.

Some historians believe that many of the present-day sports have had, at some remote time, either religious or animistic significance and are related to divination or propitiation of the spirit world. Therefore, many contemporary recreational activities are vestigial survivals of what was once useful. These activities, with some modifications, are utilized today in early education for the enhancement of perceptual development. They are used as a basis for development of skilled movements and are performed for recreational purposes.[2]

The seven movements, or movement patterns, so essential to the existence of primitive man are the basis upon which skilled movement is built. These actions, which are inherent in man, include running, jumping, climbing, lifting, carrying, hanging, and throwing. Little children can be observed to be involved in these types of activities throughout the day; they are natural, easy movements and represent the need of the organism to remain active. Throughout man's long history, such activities have formed his basic movements and have become a part of his inheritance. They represent what many authors call natural movements because they are inherent in the human organism and do not need to be taught. The job of the educator concerned primarily with behaviors in the psychomotor domain is one of building skillful efficient execution of a movement task or movement patterns upon these natural locomotor, non-locomotor, and manipulative movements.[3]

[2]Curt Sachs, *World History of the Dance* (New York: Bonanza Books, 1937), pp. 9–24.

[3]Charles C. Cowell and Frances L. Wellman, *Philosophy and Principles of Physical Education* (Englewood Cliffs, N.J.: Prentice-Hall, 1965), pp. 109–14.

In summary, it should be noted that movement in the beginning was purely an emotional phenomenon which allowed man to experience ecstasy and communion with deities. Later, movement evolved from an involuntary motor discharge to a state of frenzied movement during ceremonial rites and then to a work of art. Because movement activities were essential to both survival and communication with deities, they were paramount to the existence of man. He, therefore, began to structure his movement experiences into conscious, precise utilitarian forms. All the important events in the life cycle of primitive man, which had both practical and religious significance, were symbolized in his structured bodily movements. Man, the complicated muscular organism we know today, has progressed through a long period of evolution from a lower form of life. Throughout his evolutionary period, physical activity was essential for survival in that it was and remains important to optimum growth and development.

RATIONALE FOR THE DEVELOPMENT OF A TAXONOMY OF THE PSYCHOMOTOR DOMAIN

Movement is the key to life and exists in all areas of life. When man performs purposeful movement he is coordinating the cognitive, the psychomotor, and the affective domains. Internally, movement is continuously occurring and externally man's movement is modified by past learnings, environmental surroundings and the situation at hand. Therefore, man must be prepared to understand muscular, physiological, social, psychological and neurological movement in order to recognize and efficiently utilize the components of a movement totality.

There appears to be a growing concern for an in-depth comprehension of the child and the psychomotor domain. In some instances, educators are investigating the relationship between perceptual-motor development and academic achievement of children. The literature is replete with studies investigating meaningful play experiences and movement activities which enhance the development of spatial concepts and body control. This growing interest in psychomotor behavior will inevitably lead to a concern for explicit educational theory and meaningful efficient learning strategies to promote optimum development of each learner in the area of movement behavior.

Present-day education has a great potential for helping the learner in his "evolving" process by providing him with meaningful, sequentially organized movement activities. For the past several years, there has been a rapid development of perceptual-motor programs in elementary schools throughout the nation. These programs were originally established as therapy programs; now, however, they are utilized to provide meaningful learning experiences for populations of children with learning difficulties. The majority of these programs rely heavily upon movement activities to enhance the perceptual development of the participants.

Curricula with heavy emphasis upon specific development of desirable movement behaviors are of prime concern to early childhood educators as well as educators dealing with learning experiences in the areas of physical education, fine arts education, vocational-technical education, and special education. Research has indicated that background experiences or early learning makes a difference in later learning. If, in fact, children's past experiences do act as mediators to present learnings, then efficient utilization of the body and development of perceptual skills become paramount to the education of children. Therefore, a taxonomy for the psychomotor domain should prove beneficial to educators by helping them better understand behaviors unique to the psychomotor domain.

Since the goals of education are focused upon the growth and development of the total child, educators must become concerned with the cognitive, affective, and psychomotor behaviors. This can be accomplished by professional educators acquiring an in-depth comprehension of the child as a thinking, feeling, moving being. Without these kinds of knowledge and comprehension, educators will continue to have difficulties selecting relevant learning experiences in each of the three learning domains.

The taxonomies for the cognitive[4] and affective[5] domains were developed recently and are available for utilization by curriculum designers. These taxonomies serve as functional guides for the development of sequential goals within specific content areas. To fill a void, this taxonomy for the psychomotor domain was developed.

---

[4] Benjamin S. Bloom, ed., *Taxonomy of Educational Objectives Handbook I: Cognitive Domain* (New York: David McKay Co., 1956).

[5] David R. Krathwohl, Benjamin S. Bloom and Bertram B. Masia, *Taxonomy of Educational Objectives Handbook II: Affective Domain* (New York: David McKay Co., 1964).

The specific intent of this text is to provide a functional written taxonomy for the psychomotor domain to be utilized for the classification of observable behaviors. The classification levels within the model are hierarchical in order, arranged along a continuum for the lowest level of psychomotor behavior to the highest level. It is designed specifically to assist educators and curriculum developers to categorize relevant movement phenomenon in order to structure educational goals relevant to the needs of children.

Some educators who have utilized the taxonomies for the cognitive and affective domains to reevaluate and restructure their curricula offerings have gained new insights concerned with levels of learning and feeling. These taxonomies provided a common foundation upon which teachers could organize learning experiences for children. They enabled professionals to accurately communicate and comprehend stated educational goals. In many instances awareness of the taxonomies stimulated thoughts concerning the learning process and the problems of education. Educators have become more aware of cognitive and affective behaviors observable in children and, therefore, are now better prepared to develop curricula, instructional techniques, and measurement situations when structuring learning experiences to bring about desirable meaningful changes in children's behaviors in the two learning domains. These taxonomies have served as sources of ideas aimed at improved education for children.

Hopefully, this psychomotor taxonomy will benefit educators in much the same way as the cognitive and affective taxonomies. This taxonomy will serve to increase educators' understanding of and appreciation of meaningful movement for the total development of the child. It provides an essential framework for early childhood "readiness" programs with their predominant movement orientation. It also provides a framework for physical education programs, and can be effectively utilized for categorizing the movement behaviors essential for optimum development of children in special education programs, fine arts education and vocational-technical education. With this increased awareness of the psychomotor domain, educators will be better equipped to evaluate the numerous materials and packaged programs related to this learning domain that are currently flooding the education market. In addition, a taxonomy for this learning domain enables educators to communicate accurately their educational goals related to the psychomotor domain and facilitates the exchange of professional information regarding curriculum development in this area.

PROBLEMS INHERENT IN CLASSIFYING MOVEMENT BEHAVIORS

Since movement is incorporated in all life and is actually a prerequisite for life, it becomes a difficult task to isolate behaviors unique to the psychomotor domain. The educator understands that all behavior incorporates movement of some type, internal and external; all behaviors delve into the cognitive areas to some degree, and since man is a gregarious animal, many of his observable behaviors are modified by his affective self. But for the purposes of structuring a sequential curriculum and defining educational objectives, the educator must isolate his primary concern when studying a particular behavior; for relevant evaluations he should categorize his intended educational goal into one of the three domains. Therefore, when developing objectives for learners in the psychomotor domain, the educator should first identify the primary educational purpose for which he is writing, be it the development of manipulative and motor skills, the development of higher cognitive skills or the enhancement of the learner's self-concept.

A second problem of classifying educational objectives aimed at measuring psychomotor behavior is that a functional taxonomy of observable behaviors in this domain had not been organized as the cognitive and the affective areas had been. Kibler and others[6] stated that few psychomotor objectives were found in the literature, therefore, little work was done in organizing this domain. Perhaps it has been the lack of an organized model that contributed to the scarcity of behaviorally stated objectives. Based upon current research and comprehension of human growth and development, it must certainly be agreed that relevant opportunity for movement education beginning with early infancy is essential for optimum development in all the learning domains. Therefore, to give direction and meaning to a movement curriculum, the taxonomy for the psychomotor domain was developed to assist educators in structuring a program of movement experiences.

[6] Robert J. Kibler, Larry L. Barker and David T. Miles, *Behavioral Objectives and Instruction* (Boston: Allyn & Bacon, 1970).

Many educators have stated that the psychomotor domain is by far the easiest of all the domains for which to write educational objectives. Kibler et al.[7] state two reasons for this: first, most psychomotor behaviors are observable; and, second, most of them can be objectively measured. Nevertheless, to facilitate the development of meaningful, sequential, behaviorally stated curricula and to help better organize objective measures for educators working primarily in the psychomotor domain, the development of a workable model was essential. When educators are equipped with a usable model, it will be easier to analyze their present programs and provide learners with a balanced movement curriculum, thereby insuring relevant movement experiences at all levels of the taxonomy, rather than constantly working predominantly at the lower echelons—as has been realized upon investigation of some of the curricula where behaviorally stated objectives for the cognitive domain have been developed.

Another problem facing educators who are designing curricula is that of categorizing the behavior into one of the three domains. Educators often become confused since everything has a motor origin. In many instances, the primary concern of the educator can be logically categorized as cognitive, but he evaluates with an obvious psychomotor behavior or observable movement that the learner performs to demonstrate his understanding of a special phenomenon. This immediately raises the question: is it a psychomotor activity or a cognitive activity?

[7] Ibid.

A good example of this would be handwriting. When the student is first learning to copy, the educational intents are to provide experiences to improve the child's ability to manipulate the instrument (pencil or crayon), to improve the child's eye-hand coordination, to reinforce the concept of moving from left to right on the paper, and to improve the child's ability to form the letters or figures in legible fashion. This could be categorized as belonging to the psychomotor domain since the teacher is primarily concerned with manipulative skill and perceptual abilities. However, once the learner has mastered, to some degree, these types of skills, would it not be more logical to categorize handwriting as the learner's demonstration of his understanding of letter, word, and sentence formation? The educator must make this kind of decision. If he is measuring the content of the written work, he is obviously concerned with the cognitive aspects of the behavior. If he is measuring the actual configurations of the letters, his primary concern could well be in the psychomotor domain. This does not imply that an educator cannot be concerned with both the cognitive and the psychomotor aspects of a particular behavior; however, he must be aware of his intended goal or goals and be sure to utilize the appropriate evaluative techniques for measuring. This psychomotor taxonomy will serve as a guide for this kind of decision making. It is also extremely important for educators to comprehend the prerequisites for the development of various movement tasks. A hierarchical taxonomy provides this kind of data.

CHAPTER II

Background Information

MOVEMENT THEORIES

Before launching a discussion of models developed to facilitate the categorization of behaviors unique to the psychomotor domain, it is helpful to have some understanding of movement components and the variety of ways authors have analyzed and categorized movement.

In the literature on movement, many terms are used synonymously; *motor* and *movement* are but two of them. Kephart[1] distinguishes between *movement* and *motor*, calling *movement*, any external observable motion and *motor*, the internal efferent impulses. Internal motor activity is constantly occurring while observable movement or movement patterns such as walking and object-manipulation are not.

If *movement* is viewed as a design that is created in space, it can be categorized as either non-locomotor movement, observable response performed by the body in a stationary position such as clapping, or locomotor movement, observable responses of the body moving in space from one point to another such as skipping. If *movement* is viewed muscularly, it can be divided into three categories: (1) flexion, which is the act of muscle

---

[1] N. E. Kephart, *The Slow Learner in the Classroom* (Columbus, Ohio: Charles E. Merrill, 1960), pp. 35–53.

contraction causing a bending movement; (2) extension, which is a straightening or a return movement from flexion; and (3) rotation. However, most movement patterns are a combination of the three muscle movements.

The three types of basic *movement* as identified by physicists are (1) translational motion where all parts of the moving body have the same velocity and direction; (2) rotational motion where the body moves in concentric circles about an axis; and (3) oscillational motion where a body swings back and forth between fixed limits.

The term *motor*, which is used by most writers, connotes to most readers that a motor response is an observable movement response to a stimulus. For the purposes of reporting the literature in this text, *motor* and *movement* are used interchangeably; however, Kephart's explicit distinction should be kept in mind.

Smith and Smith[2] categorized *movement* into three major areas. The first they called postural movement, which regulates body positioning. The second category encompassed travel or locomotor movements, and the third category included manipulative movements. These subcategories of *movement* do not differ drastically from Kephart's definition of *movement*, with the exception of the first subcategory. Smith and Smith must have been referring to dynamic posture because there are many postural adjustments made internally causing only slight body sway which is almost nondetectable.

[2] K. U. Smith and W. H. Smith, *Perception and Motor* (Philadelphia: W. B. Saunders, 1962).

Stone[3] organized movement behaviors into five categories. However, these categories dealt with types of force involved in the movement. The first category is labeled *maximum force impulse*, the second, *slow tension movement*, and the third, *rapid tension*. Categories four and five are labeled *ballistic* and *oscillating movements* respectively.

Scott[4] divided *movement* into four types: *precision skills*, *pushing-pulling movements*, *throwing movements*, and *striking movements*. She further classified specific skill movements into preparatory movement, action, and follow-through.

Hartson's[5] classification system deals first with basic posture, then ballistic movements involving locomotion, upper limbs, and lower limbs, next vocal movements, and last eye movements.

Some authors have gone a step beyond merely classifying *movement*; they have developed models to explain movement behaviors, factors that modify movement performance, and components essential to the development of efficient movement skills.

A new conceptualization for the art and science of human movement presented by Abernathy and Waltz[6]

[3] H. Stone, *Applied Anatomy and Kinesiology* (Philadelphia: Lea and Febiger, 1953).

[4] Gladys M. Scott, *Analysis of Human Motion* (New York: Appleton-Century-Crofts, 1963).

[5] L. D. Hartson, "Contrasting Approaches to the Analysis of Skilled Movements," *Journal of General Psychology*, vol. 20 (1939):280–82.

[6] Ruth Abernathy and Maryann Waltz, "Art and Science of Human Movement," *Quest II: The Art and Science of Human Movement*, The National Association for Physical Education of College Women and the National College Physical Education Association for Men, (April 1964), 1–7.

encompasses the psychological, the physiological, and the social aspects of movement activities. They contended that human movement is purpose-oriented being initiated by the learner in an effort to achieve a desired objective, to communicate an idea or concept, to express a feeling or emotion and to relate the self to the surrounding environment and peer group. Though human movement is product-oriented, it is, nevertheless, restricted by the level of ability traits of the functional body, and the limits of physical laws of motion which include equilibrium, motion, and force.

Since *movement* does not occur in a vacuum, there are many interactions within the individual and his environment which act as modifiers to human movement. These are divided in the Abernathy-Waltz model into five categories. These categories are called: *movement experiences, personality structure, personal perceptions, social cultural environment,* and *physical environment.*

Barsch's[7] *movigenics* theory appears to be a theory of movement efficiency aimed at optimal survival of the individual. The developmental task for the performer is to become an efficient mover in all segments of space to promote his optimal survival. He divided space into three territories, the domain, the fields, and the zones. The challenge for the learner in each territory is to achieve grace, comfort, ease, and efficiency of movement. It is through exploration of these territories that the learner goes from the naive to the sophisticated performer. The learner's spatial terrains expand with the

[7] Ray H. Barsch, *Achieving Perceptual-Motor Efficiency, A Space-Oriented Approach to Learning* (Seattle, Washington: Seattle Sequin School, 1967).

increased mobility which comes with maturation and growth.

The domains of space are four in number in this theory. The first, termed *milieu interior*, refers to the human physiological system or internal environment. The main concern of this domain is the development of efficient functioning within the individual. *Physical space* refers to the observable world of objects and events; it is the second domain. The third domain, *milieu space*, is the space of social identification, and the fourth domain, termed *cognitive space*, encompasses the terrains of symbols, thoughts, ideas, and conceptualizations.

The six fields of space in which the learner can explore for further sophistication are listed by Barsch as right and left fields, front and back fields and up and down fields. These fields are always relative to the position of the performer. Barsch's six fields of space are termed *directionality* by some authors.

The zones of space are defined as being near-space, mid-space, far-space, and remote-space. Near-space is the basic zone of performance with boundaries extended approximately two feet away from the performer's body. It is the area for manipulative tasks including reaching, grasping, and releasing.

Once the individual is capable of propulsion, he begins exploring mid-space, which has a measurable distance of from two to sixteen feet in all directions. Far-space is the designation given to the third zone of space and encompasses a distance of seventeen to thirty feet. Barsch also terms this the zone of extension since the performer must remove himself a considerable distance from his primary base of near support. Any distance beyond thirty feet is considered to be the fourth zone designated remote-space. It is the terrain of perspectives, goals, objectives, and ambitions.

Barsch lists three main components of movement efficiency: postural-transport orientation, percepto-cognitive, and degrees of freedom. The postural-transport orientation component encompasses five subcomponents of muscular strength, dynamic balance, body awareness, spatial awareness, and temporal awareness. These five subcomponents are related to the basic problem of moving in the environment and each represents a fundamental unit required of a dynamic mobile performer. They are considered to be essential to the organization of motion, and in fact set the foundation for the quality of *movement* the performer will be capable of achieving.

The percepto-cognitive mode component encompasses six subcomponents that are gustatory, olfactory, tactual, kinesthetic, auditory and visual senses. It is through these modes that the performer acquires information about the environment to organize his movements and control his behavior. These six subcomponents are designed to implement the organization of the first major component by adding what Barsch calls meaning to *movement.*

The third component of movement efficiency is listed as degrees of freedom. This component encompasses four subcomponents of bilaterality, rhythm, flexibility, and motor planning. The subcomponents within this category are said to enhance and enrich the quality of movement that the performer is capable of achieving.

Thus the key to Barsch's *movigenics* theory is movement efficiency. The principal challenge for educators who desire to optimize human development is identified by Barsch as helping each individual discover how to move with the greatest possible efficiency. This, though interesting, in no way helps the educator categorize movement behaviors.

Hunt[8] proposed a model of movement behavior that takes a gestalt view of man and the way in which he organizes and expresses his energy systems. It contends that man develops a style of moving based upon how he uses force, its shape in space, and the time it takes. Interpretation of stimuli comes from the organization of perceptions and the concepts developed. The perceptual process and the resulting concepts which develop, make it possible for the learner to define, integrate, and understand his own living body that interacts with environmental forces. The framework of Hunt's model arises from figure-ground discriminations, the concept of laterality, and emotional perceptual organization, and from space-time, weight, and body image concepts. Hunt proposed that basic movement experiences must be continued systematically throughout life to facilitate the development of skilled movement. A learner's basic effort patterns must be mastered before he can master a complex skill or movement pattern. The ultimate goal of this experience approach would be for the learner to develop a broad movement repertoire along with the

[8] Valerie Hunt, "Movement Behavior: A Model for Action," *Quest II: The Art and Science of Human Movement*, The National Association for Physical Education of College Women and the National College Physical Education Association for Men (April 1964):57–66.

skills of feeling and analyzing his own movement. It would put the learner at the center of the process, and eventually make him his own teacher.

Cratty[9] developed a three-factor theory of perceptual-motor behavior. The base of this theory is entitled General Supports of Behavior. Into this category are placed such characteristics as (1) level of aspiration, (2) level of persistence, (3) level of arousal/motivation, (4) ability to analyze the mechanics of a task, and (5) various perceptual abilities. These qualities, though relatively fixed, can be modified or influenced by individual experiences. Cratty contends that these attributes are influential in a variety of human behaviors.

The second level reported by Cratty is that of ability traits. In this category are listed such traits as strength, endurance, flexibility, speed, balance, and coordination. These are all traits which each individual can develop to his potential and which influence his perceptual motor performance.

The third level is listed as factors specific to the task and situation. Examples of these are the energy demands required of the task, the values the performer places upon the task, the past experiences and the social characteristics of the performance situation. The actual observable psychomotor behavior appears at the third level or apex of the triangle described by Cratty. It is at this level that behavioral objectives could be constructed for the specific skills (tasks) the learner will be required to perform.

[9] Bryant J. Cratty, *Movement Behavior and Motor Learning* (Philadelphia: Lea and Febiger, 1964), pp. 75–98.

The above models for skill development do not lend themselves to assisting the behavioral objective writer or the curriculum developer in categorizing behaviors in the psychomotor domain. They all appear to deal primarily with the learning of a specific movement or skill, rather than with providing a framework for a movement hierarchy.

MODELS FOR CLASSIFYING PSYCHOMOTOR BEHAVIORS

One of the first models to be developed to help teachers and curriculum developers to classify behaviors in the psychomotor domain was organized by Ragsdale.[10] He stated that every class subject and extra-curricular activity included motor behavior of some type that was the most important activity to be learned. In other words, he asserted that all subject areas have behaviors indicative of the three learning domains. He categorized motor activities into three main areas. Object-motor activities was the first major area. Behaviors classified in this area are directed primarily toward manipulating or acting with direct reference to an object. The criteria for judging skill attainment in this area are listed as speed and precision with which results are obtained.

The second major area in Ragsdale's division of motor activities was language-motor activities. In this

---

[10]C. E. Ragsdale, "How Children Learn Motor Types of Activities," *Learning and Instruction*, Forty-ninth Yearbook of the National Society for the Study of Education (1950):69–91.

group he listed movements of speech organs, eye-movements and movement involved in handwriting. The performance of motor activities in this category has symbolic value, being primarily concerned with recording, receiving, or communicating ideas. Here, skilled bodily movements are utilized to construct symbols.

Feeling-motor activities is the third category. The primary concerns in this major area are the communication of attitudes, feelings, and emotions through the medium of movement. The subject area examples listed for this division are dance, fine arts, and music—both instrumental and vocal.

Another model for classifying behaviors in the psychomotor domain was prepared by Simpson.[11] Her model has seven hierarchical classification levels with each one containing several subcategories. The model was developed as a taxonomy with the first level being perception, which deals with sensory stimulation, cue selection and translation. Level two is labeled set, dealing with mental, physical, and emotional set. The third level, guided response, deals with imitation and trial and error learning. Mechanism is the label for level four, and it deals with the mechanics and habituation of movement. Levels five, six and seven are labeled complex overt response, adaptation, and origination respectively.

The first two levels, taking the learner from stimulation to stimulus interpretation through set or readiness for response, are not readily observable behaviors. The

[11] Elizabeth Jane Simpson, "The Classification of Educational Objectives: Psychomotor Domain," University of Illinois Research Project No. OE 5, (1966):85–104.

next three levels can actually be categorized as a learning sequence inherent in many motor skills. When first learning a motor skill, a child goes through imitative movements and much trial and error learning. Once a certain confidence has been achieved by the learner in the performance of the skill, it becomes what Simpson terms mechanized or habitual. As the learner proceeds through the learning sequence, hopefully, he attains a higher level of skill in performing the motor skill. This is categorized in the Simpson schema as the fifth level, complex overt response. The last two levels of the schema, adaptation and origination, can be interpreted as refinement of basic motor responses and the creation of new aesthetic movement patterns. Though this is a fine model, it limits the behavioral objective writer or curriculum designer to the last three levels for classification of behaviors since levels one and two are not observable responses, and levels three and four are inherent within sequential learning of a specific motor skill, and at this point in motor skill learning a learner is not ready for evaluation since he is still acquiring the skill. Levels five, six, and seven, though observable, reflect the degree of skill and creative levels the learner has attained.

Simpson's model could be utilized when analyzing one particular movement skill a student is attempting to learn and master. He goes through the phase of interpreting the stimulus (perception); he then prepares himself for active response (set); since the skilled movement is new to him, he must first imitate what he perceives the task or movement to be. After some imitation, the learner practices the movement going through trial and error learning. Once he has some confidence in his performance of the movement, according to Simpson's model, he is at the mechanism level, in other words, his movement pattern becomes habitual, progressing into a smooth complex overt response. When the learner has mastered the skilled movement he is able to modify it (adaptation), and then to create movement patterns based upon his acquired skilled movement (origination).

The Kibler, Barker, Miles[12] model for classification of behaviors in the psychomotor domain is divided into four major categories. These classifications were not intended to be taxonomic. The divisions include behaviors of gross bodily movement, finely coordinated movements, non-verbal communications and speech behaviors. The first three categories represent observable movement phenomena. The fourth category represents oral responses from the learner, and instead of becoming a visual stimulus for the evaluator as movement responses are, it becomes for the evaluator an auditory stimulus.

The first category encompasses locomotor and non-locomotor skills; the second category includes manipulative skills and visual-motor coordination skills. The third category though including observable phenomena, does not appear to fit in the psychomotor domain as a major category. The subcategories of facial expression and gestures actually reflect an interest or attitude toward something and as such are not offered in a curriculum as prime concerns, with the exception,

---

[12] Robert J. Kibler, Larry L. Barker and David T. Miles, *Behavioral Objectives and Instruction* (Boston: Allyn & Bacon, 1970).

perhaps, of a drama class. Non-verbal communication through bodily movements is an activity performed by all learners and is indicative of a mood, emotion or self-concept. Even though all of these subcategories are included as part of a specialized curriculum such as theater or creative dance, do they really belong as a major category in the psychomotor domain? If a learner is not formally trained in these areas of non-verbal communication, would they not be better utilized as unobtrusive measures which communicate to the teacher the attitude or value a learner places upon some activity or event? The fourth category deals with sound production, sound-word formation, and sound-gesture coordination which are not all observable phenomena. The movement per se would not be evaluated, but rather the result of the movement. Though these are all essential behaviors, it would be difficult to categorize some of them into particular domains.

To facilitate summarization of the three models for classifying behaviors in the psychomotor domain, Figure 1 is provided. The reader should note the similarities of Ragsdale's object-motor category and Kibler's finely coordinated category. There also appears to be a definite similarity between Ragsdale's language-motor and Kibler's speech behavior category, and between Ragsdale's feeling-motor and Kibler's non-verbal category. Any manipulative, locomotor or non-locomotor skill performed by a learner would be placed in Simpson's complex overt response category. Her complex overt response category appears to correspond to Ragsdale's object-motor and Kibler's gross body and finely coordinated categories. Simpson's adaptation and origina-

Ragsdale	Simpson	Kibler, et al.
NON-TAXONOMIC	TAXONOMIC	NON-TAXONOMIC
1. Object Motor (manipulating or acting with direct reference to an object)	1. Perception (interpreting)	1. Gross Body Movements (locomotor and axile)
	2. Set (preparing)	
2. Language Motor (movements of speech, sight, handwriting)	3. Guided Response (learning)	2. Finely Coordinated (manipulation and visual motor coordination)
	4. Mechanism (habituating)	
3. Feeling Motor (movements communicating feelings and attitudes)	5. Complex Overt Response (performing)	3. Non-Verbal (communicating feelings and attitude)
	6. Adaptation (modifying)	4. Speech Behaviors
	7. Origination (creating)	

Figure 1—A Comparative View of Three Models for Classifying Psychomotor Behaviors.

tion categories also correspond to Ragsdale's feeling-motor.

Utilizing an eye-hand coordination skill of catching a ball, one should be able to speculate as to the categorization each author might give to this particular skill, using his own model. Since ball catching is a skill where the learner is engaged in an activity with direct reference to an object, Ragsdale would categorize it as object-motor, Simpson would probably categorize it as complex overt response, and Kibler might categorize it as finely coordinated movement since it involves visual-motor coordination.

A dance-walk which is a basic skill in beginning modern dance classes, would be categorized by Ragsdale in his feeling-motor category. Since the skill is not a creative one but is a modification of walking, Simpson would probably categorize the dance-walk in her adaptation category, and because the dance-walk is a locomotor skill, Kibler would probably categorize it as gross body movement.

SUMMARY

Prior to designing a behaviorally stated psychomotor curriculum, certain basic understandings are essential. First, problems will definitely arise when an educator first begins to categorize learner behaviors into one of the three learning domains. To minimize the problem, he should ask himself, "What is my primary concern or intended educational goal?" If the educator can actually label his primary concern as a manipulative or movement behavior change which he is attempting to bring about in the learner, he can place his educational goal in the psychomotor domain and begin searching for a relevant evaluation of the stated goal. The educator, however, must realize that some educational goals will have cognitive, psychomotor and affective aspects. In this case, he must be sure he evaluates each aspect of the stated educational goal.

Secondly, the educator should now be aware that the fundamental movement patterns are inherent within the individual, but there still exists the need for learning experiences to enhance the development of movement skills. It is through continued practice and meaningful movement experiences that the learner facilitates the enrichment of his perceptual abilities. The educator should be aware of the developmental theories of Hebb and Piaget in which both place quantity of stimulation above quality during the first two years of life. However, the qualitative aspects of stimulation become essential by at least four years of age and are most beneficial if directly related to the behavior to be changed.

Thirdly, the educator should be aware that a great deal of quality work has been done in the study and organization of movement behaviors. This chapter reports only a small portion of the literature to provide some insights into the area of movement. There are, however, only a few models designed specifically for the categorization of behaviors in the psychomotor domain, and few of these are truly functional. The model developed in this book is submitted as a functional model that can be utilized by the research worker, the curriculum designer, and the classroom teacher.

In an educational setting the overlap of the domains is obvious; children learn and function as an entity. To make the educational experiences meaningful to children, the educator must select relevant educational goals in each of the three learning domains. He must structure his curriculum sequentially and should develop his intended goals in behavioral terms. His teaching strategies should be relevant to the learning styles of his children and his educational goals related to pupil needs and stated educational goals.

When the educator understands the principles and theories upon which this psychomotor taxonomy must out of necessity be structured, some basic comprehensions regarding the components of movement theory, and the procedures for learning a movement skill, he will be better prepared to organize a meaningful sequential movement curriculum, will be equipped to classify psychomotor behaviors and will be more informed regarding the selection of reliable measurement techniques.

One must always keep in mind that behavior may be conceptualized as falling into one of three learning domains, but in reality, when observing a child's behavior it is usually a combination of all three. Nevertheless, in order to effectively study and bring about desirable behavior change, educators must isolate behavior into component parts. In order to write relevant behavior objectives, the educator must focus upon the primary concern and categorize objectives into one of the three domains. He must also be aware that almost every curriculum will have stated objectives in all the domains. But in order to facilitate the development of explicit objectives in the psychomotor domain that are in fact relevant to the intended curriculum rather than being an exercise in mental gymnastics, the writer must have some basic understandings regarding the functioning of the organism, the components of movement theory and the procedures for learning a movement skill.

CHAPTER III

The Taxonomy for the Psychomotor Domain

INTRODUCTION

The explanation of the term psychomotor given in Krathwohl's taxonomy states that this particular area should be concerned with manipulative skills, motor skills, and acts requiring neuromuscular coordination.[1] Oversimplified, neuromuscular coordination is the team work or efficiency between nerve impulse and muscle contraction and logically cannot be considered a major subcategory under the psychomotor domain since it is inherent within the first two subcategories. In other words, motor skills and manipulative skills both require neuromuscular coordination. Kraus[2] defined man as motion, and most people interpret psychomotor as dealing with observable human motion. When the term is separated into its two component parts, psycho and motor, it connotes mind-movement or voluntary motion. Therefore, as an operational definition, the term psychomotor should communicate to the reader that all observable voluntary human motion will fall into the learning domain. The unique characteristic of all behav-

---

[1] David R. Krathwohl, Benjamin S. Bloom and Bertram B. Masia, *Taxonomy of Educational Objectives Handbook II: Affective Domain* (New York: David McKay Co., 1964).
    [2] Hans Kraus, *Hypokinetic Disease* (Springfield, Ill.: Thomas, 1961), p. 8.

iors which will be categorized in the psychomotor domain is that they will be observable voluntary actions or action patterns performed by the learner and designated by the educator as being an essential portion of the educational goal of his particular curriculum.

With the above understanding of psychomotor behaviors, the reader is better prepared to explore the taxonomy dealing with these behaviors. The classification levels are intended to be hierarchical in order, arranged along a continuum from lowest level of observable movement behavior to highest level. The reader should be aware, however, that in some instances there will also be continuums existing within a classification level. These will be clearly explained in the description of each classification in the taxonomy.

1.00 Reflex Movements
2.00 Basic-Fundamental Movements
3.00 Perceptual Abilities
4.00 Physical Abilities
5.00 Skilled Movements
6.00 Non-Discursive Communication

Figure 2—Classification Levels of the Psychomotor Domain

Each section contains a brief description of the classification level and, where necessary, of the corresponding subcategories. In some instances illustrative behavioral objectives are stated to further clarify the types of movement tasks that could appropriately be placed within the classification level and the subcategories. This does not imply that each subcategory is mutually exclusive; there is some overlap, and therefore, it is possible that the reader will be able to appropriately change the location of some of the example objectives.

The reader should keep in mind that this scheme was designed specifically to assist educators and curriculum developers to categorize observable movement phenomenon into one of the six hierarchical levels of the psychomotor domain.

Figure 2 is the basic framework for this proposed model for classifying observable movement behaviors in the psychomotor domain. Acting as a basis for all movement behavior is the first category, reflex movements, and the second category, basic or fundamental movement patterns, is actually the combining of reflex movements into inherent movement patterns. The learner responds involuntarily in the first category and though the movement patterns in the second category are inherent within the learner, he utilizes these patterns during voluntary movement. It is upon these voluntary movement patterns that he builds his skilled movements. The next two categories, perceptual abilities and physical abilities, are further developed through maturation and learning. The learner goes through many learning experiences that sharpen his perceptual abilities, and engages in many activities that increase the quality of his physical abilities. The efficiency and degree of skilled movement attained by any learner is based upon the learner's control of his basic or fundamental movements, the degree of efficiency with which he perceives stimuli, and the level of development he has attained in the fourth category of physical abilities. Once the learner has acquired a skilled movement vocabulary he has the necessary tools (an efficient body—an accurate perceptual system—and skilled movement repertoire) for modifying and creating aesthetic movement patterns.

The top category is the highest degree of skill attainment the learner can achieve. The reader, however, must be aware that a continuum exists in both category five, skilled movement, and category six, non-discursive communication. In other words, there are degrees or levels of skilled movement a learner can attain and also degrees or levels of creativity learners are capable of achieving.

The learner builds upon the existing structure. To attain creative aesthetic movement patterns (observable phenomena), he must have developed the essential prerequisites from the skilled movements, physical abilities, and perceptual abilities categories, and must possess the basic innate movement patterns and adequately functioning reflexes from the lower two categories.

Since the child comes into the world possessing the movement phenomena which are characteristic of the first two categories, these types of movement are not part of the planned school curriculum. Therefore, teachers would not be concerned about writing educational objectives for these two categories of the psychomotor domain. The only exception to this would possibly be in a physical therapy program where reeducation of the basic locomotor movements is part of the planned curriculum. In that case, educational objectives for each therapy patient could be written for the second category incorporating all innate movement patterns.

Perceptual abilities, being an out-growth of both neurological maturation and past learning experiences, are usually developed to some degree when the child enters school. However, due to lack of meaningful early childhood experiences and varying rates of maturation and growth, many preschoolers or primary children are in need of structured perceptual-motor programs to enhance the development of these perceptual abilities which are in fact prerequisites to learning in each of the three domains. Some investigators claim a direct relationship exists between efficient performance of a movement skill and the learner's perceptual abilities. It is at this point in the model, perceptual abilities, that most educators will begin writing educational objectives. Educators dealing with handicapped children, however, will more than likely begin at the second level. Each child, in order to achieve movement efficiency, must have adequately functioning perceptual abilities. These abilities are essential for efficient interpretation of stimuli.

Though the act of perceiving (stimulus interpretation) is not directly observable, there are observable phenomena which reflect this perceptual act. Therefore, if the outcomes of perception are viewed, the particular modality becomes the learning task, and the observable outcome which reflects the perceptual act becomes the learner performance of the behavioral objective. An illustration will perhaps clarify this point. In most perceptual-motor programs, figure-ground differentiation is a perceptual ability utilizing the visual mode. A teacher may state his goal in either of two ways, utilizing the perceptual ability as the learning task or the specific component of the perceptual ability which is of prime concern.

Goal: To develop the visual discrimination of preschool children

or
Goal: *To develop the figure-ground differentiation abilities of*
preschool children.

When the writer adds the evaluation statement to his
goal statement, it will be the observable outcome of the
learner's perceptual abilities.

If visual discrimination is utilized as the learning
task the evaluation statement would incorporate several
learner performances since visual discrimination as defined in this text is composed of several subcategories.

Behavioral Objective:

To develop the visual discriminatory abilities of preschool
children as measured by

a. each child's ability to select, without error, all the
circles from a group of ten cardboard figures,

b. each child's ability to picture-read from left to right,
without error, a series of three one-line picture stories,

c. each child's ability to recall from memory and reproduce at least two of the three figures, circle, square,
triangle and

d. each child's ability to successfully bounce, without
error, a playground ball five times in succession.

The reader should recognize in the above illustration that the evaluation included some form of measurement or performance on the child's part for four of the
components of visual discrimination. The ability to differentiate between objects is a measure of visual acuity;
to picture read from left to right is a form of visual
tracking; to recall a previously viewed group of figures is
visual memory, and to bounce a ball successfully is a
measure of figure-ground discrimination along with eye-
hand coordination.

If figure-ground differentiation, which is a subcategory of visual discrimination, is used as the learning task, the evaluation statement need not be so inclusive, and can in fact be a more intense measure of the learner's specific ability.

Behavioral Objective:

To develop the figure-ground differentiation abilities of preschool children as determined by each child's ability to successfully bounce, without missing, a playground ball five times in succession and to successfully catch, at least three out of five times, a playground ball that has been thrown from a distance of approximately ten feet.

The reader is probably thinking that ball bouncing does not involve only the child's ability to select the dominant figure from the surrounding background, but also involves eye-hand coordination, and that is correct. Nevertheless, because the learner must be able to perceive the ball before he can catch it, this activity can be one of those used to evaluate the learner's figure-ground differentiation abilities.

Cautions

A learner's behaviors do not fall neatly into one of the three separate compartments of the learning domains. The learner behaves as an integrated whole and the behavioral objective writer must isolate the particular behavior which, at the moment, is his prime concern, being careful, however, not to lose the values from the other aspects of the learner's behavior. Even within the categorical classification levels of the psychomotor domain the reader must be aware that some behaviors could probably be appropriately categorized in one of two classification levels.

Perhaps an illustration or two will be useful here. For the "normal" learner in a primary class, walking would be considered a basic or fundamental movement and, therefore, categorized in the 2.00 classification level, basic or fundamental movement. There may be, however, an instance, while dealing with a therapy patient or a child with a motor handicap, when walking can actually be labeled as a movement requiring a great deal of practice and effort on the part of the learner. Logically, for that particular type of learner, the writer would be tempted to categorize it as a skilled movement; however, the movement still represents a basic or fundamental movement pattern, even though the learner had to practice intensively to acquire the movement.

Another situation that could cause some confusion would be the movement exploration activities of primary children. Suppose, for purposes of illustration, that a preschool child is exploring his movement potential based upon his basic-fundamental movement pattern of walking. Since the child is exploring variations of the walking pattern and no practice for a particular pattern has occurred, this could be categorized as the beginnings of creative movements. This example should point out to the reader that it is possible for preschoolers and primary children to reach the lower levels of the continuum in classification level six, non-discursive communicative movement, when they begin exploring the ranges of movement variations they are capable of performing.

This in no way destroys the hierarchical order of the scheme simply because, to reach the highest levels of the continuum within the sixth classification level, the learner must progress through each level developing proficiencies within each level upon which to build the movement repertoire.

Now that it is established that there will be accompanying affective and cognitive behaviors in any of the learner's psychomotor behaviors that have been selected for observation, and that occasionally a behavioral objective writer may be confronted with the decision of behavior placement within this particular psychomotor scheme, the reader will be led down one more side-path to refresh his memory of early child development.

A View of the "Standard Model"

The educator must understand the equipment that comes with the standard model, the learner. If the educator does not possess this basic understanding of where the "normal" learner is in regard to movement behavior, he will be unable to structure relevant movement experiences for the learner in order to take him from a known to an unknown movement pattern. Without this basic knowledge, it is possible to be caught up in the trap of writing behavioral objectives for behaviors that could logically be categorized as psychomotor but which are, in fact, predominantly cognitive. A case in point will clarify this last important concept. A chemistry teacher has, as a primary concern or goal, the mixing of specific chemicals to satisfy various experiments. Though the actual pouring of specific liquids into the container takes fine motor coordination consisting of a kinesthetic awareness for lightness of touch and the manipulation of equipment, these are not skilled movements being taught to the learner. They are basic or fundamental movements the learner possesses and practices early in life. The primary concern or goal of the chemistry teacher is cognitive. He wants the learner to understand the reactions that occur upon mixing various chemicals, and he requests the learner to perform the psychomotor act of mixing chemicals as one measure of the learner's cognition of chemicals and their corresponding reactions.

With this in mind, a brief sketch of Gesell's[3] stages of motor development will provide a basic understanding of the "equipment that comes with the standard model."

During the first four weeks, the learner is an immobile individual who during his waking hours displays the tonic-neck-reflex attitude. This tonic-neck-reflex, occasionally called the "fencing position," is the ground work for the total reaction system. The tonic-neck-reflex attitude can be observed when viewing an infant lying on his back with one arm flexed and the opposite arm extended with the head turned toward the outstretched or extended arm.

The learner's head becomes more mobile and he begins to correlate the movement of his arms and hands with the position of his head and eyes at approximately sixteen weeks of age. He begins bilaterally reaching for

---

[3] Arnold Gesell, *First Five Years of Life* (New York: Harper, 1940), pp. 10–57.

viewed objects using massive movements involving the head, shoulders and arms.

At approximately twenty-eight weeks, he is able to sit and his prehensory approach (reaching) toward viewed objects becomes more one-sided as opposed to the bilateral prehensory approach of the earlier period. Not only does he reach for an object, he can grasp, transfer from one hand to the other, and manipulate the objects.

By the time the learner reaches forty weeks of age, his sitting equilibrium is mastered and he is able to stand supported. He becomes more skillful at using his index finger and thumb thus showing refined prehensory movements.

At approximately the age of one, he creeps efficiently. He supports himself in an erect position and by fifteen months he is capable of walking independently. His prehensory patterns are precise and he is almost capable of voluntary release. He now is able to manipulate a ball and blocks and if given a writing implement such as a crayon, he is able to scribble.

When the learner reaches the age of two, he can run. He is capable of walking up and down stairs, and can even jump down from the first step. He appears to have a "motor mania," enjoying all of the physical activity he can obtain. His manual repertoire by the age of two has increased and includes such activities as turning pages of a book, building a block tower, snipping with scissors (not cutting), stringing beads, holding a glass of milk, and folding paper.

By the age of three, the learner has sophisticated his fine manipulative movements of making controlled marks. He is not yet able to draw a man, but does demonstrate more control in his drawing strokes. His locomotor movements are also more refined. He can accelerate and decelerate with ease while running and can make sudden stops and turn sharper corners. He now uses an alternating foot pattern, can jump down a stair with both feet together, and can peddle a bicycle. He is also capable of balancing on one foot momentarily, and jumping upward.

By the age of five the learner has a well-developed sense of equilibrium which is obvious in his locomotor movements and body posture. He is capable of hopping and skipping, displaying a good deal of motor control.

His manual controls have improved in the past year. Not only is he capable of dressing himself, undressing himself and lacing his shoes, he can now also tie his shoes. He is more efficient when manipulating his toothbrush and comb. He can draw a recognizable man and demonstrate greater efficiency when copying figures of a circle, square, and triangle. He still, however, has difficulty copying a diamond.

Gesell[4] outlines four basic principles relating to the development of movement behavior early in the life of the learner. First, movement development occurs in a cephalo-caudal direction; in other words, the learner first performs movements of the head and trunk area progressing down to his feet. He views and reaches before he walks. Second, movement develops proximodistally—the learner first explores movement with large

[4]Arnold Gesell, "The Ontogenesis of Infant Behavior," ed., Leonard Carmichael, *Manual of Child Psychology* (New York: John Wiley and Sons, 1946), pp. 295–331.

shoulder and trunk muscles before he develops movements of the forearms and hands. Third, movement of the hands progresses from grasping and clasping to precise manipulative abilities, from the outside of the hand to the inside of the hand. The fourth principle states that movement develops as a reciprocal neuromotor interweaving—movement behavior develops not as a climbing upward from one step to another but as an interweaving of behaviors which gives the learner an appearance of advancing and then slightly regressing. Anyone who has observed a learner during the first fifteen months of life should have noted that though he has learned to walk he occasionally reverts to creeping; his movement behavior vascillates from bipedal to quadrupedal.

With this view of the "standard model," it is important to keep in mind that individual differences in the development of movement behavior are many and varied; some occur simply because children have progressed differently in growth and maturation.

It should be obvious that when the "standard model" walks through the kindergarten doorway he should have with him a basic reflex system which has given way to a well developed motor system manifested through a variety of controlled locomotor, non-locomotor, and manipulative movements. His perceptual abilities, which have been developing through maturation and learning since the first four weeks of life when he began his initial practices, utilizing his visual, auditory, and kinesthetic modalities, are ready for further sophistication. Occasionally the "model" or learner who walks through the door to formal education does not have all the essential "equipment" and therefore must have an individualized program developed to assist him in obtaining all the prerequisites to efficient functioning in the psychomotor as well as the cognitive and affective domains of learning.

Classification Level One—Reflex Movements

Reflex movements or actions are elicited in response to some stimulus without conscious volition on the part of the learner. They are not voluntary movements but may be considered as an essential base for movement behavior.

Though educators or curriculum developers will not be concerned with writing behavioral objectives for this particular classification level, it is included in the taxonomy for classifying behaviors in the psychomotor domain because reflex movements are actually prerequisites to development in the following classification levels.

Figure 3 divides observable movement into two categories, involuntary and voluntary. The first classification level, reflex movements, contains two major divisions, spinal reflexes and suprasegmental reflexes. Spinal reflexes are further subdivided into segmental and intersegmental reflexes. Segmental reflexes are those which occur over pathways of one spinal segment and intersegmental reflexes are those which involve more than one spinal segment. The suprasegmental reflexes involve the participation of the brain.[5]

[5]Clifford T. Morgan, "Motor Functions," *Physiological Psychology* (New York: McGraw-Hill, 1965), pp. 272–305.

The second division is voluntary purposeful movement. The types of movements listed are those found in the second classification level, basic-fundamental movements, and will be explained in detail at a later point in this chapter.

Observable Movement	
INVOLUNTARY REFLEX MOVEMENTS	VOLUNTARY PURPOSEFUL MOVEMENTS

1. Spinal Reflexes
    Segmental
    Intersegmental
2. Suprasegmental Reflexes
    Extensor Rigidity
    Plasticity Reactions
    Postural Reflexes
	1. Locomotor
	
	2. Non-Locomotor
	
	3. Manipulative

Figure 3—Two Major Types of Movement Responses

The first classification level, reflex movements, is the first category in the model.

> 1.00   Reflex Movements
> > 1.10   Segmental Reflexes
> > > 1.11   Flexion Reflex
> > > 1.12   Myotatic Reflex
> > > 1.13   Extensor Reflex
> > > 1.14   Crossed Extension Reactions
> >
> > 1.20   Intersegmental Reflexes
> > > 1.21   Cooperative Reflex
> > > 1.22   Competitive Reflex
> > > 1.23   Successive Induction
> > > 1.24   Reflex Figure
> >
> > 1.30   Suprasegmental Reflexes
> > > 1.31   Extensor Rigidity
> > > 1.32   Plasticity Reactions

    1.33 Postural Reflexes
        1.331 Supporting Reactions
        1.332 Shifting Reactions
        1.333 Tonic-Attitudinal Reflexes
        1.334 Righting Reactions
        1.335 Grasp Reflex
        1.336 Placing and Hopping Reactions

1.00 Reflex Movements are those movements which are involuntary in nature. They are functional at birth, developing through maturation. They are the precursors of basic or fundamental movement.

    1.10 Segmental Reflexes are those reflex movements which involve one spinal segment.

        1.11 Flexion Reflex is a response that involves the limbs, arms or legs. It is a movement which causes the limb to move towards the body and away from the ground. This response is utilized to avoid or escape harmful or threatening stimuli and it occurs in response to pain. An example of the flexion reflex would be a child bending at the hip joint, ducking the head, and flexing the arms in a protective movement to avoid being hit by an oncoming object.

        1.12 Myotatic, or Stretch Reflex, as it is sometimes called, is a fine balancing mechanism. This reflex causes an increased tension in the extensor muscles—antigravity muscles—which support the learner's body. It is a postural reflex because it maintains a slight tension, facilitating adjustment in static balance. It is in part responsible for the balanced control which helps the learner to maintain his center of gravity within the limits of his base of support.

1.13 Extensor Reflex is a reaction of a limb. It is observed as a limb straightening out to support the body against gravity. It comes into play whenever the pressure receptors on the soles of the feet come in contact with the ground. Therefore, it becomes activated during such locomotor movements as walking or running.

1.14 Crossed Extension Reaction is another type of extensor reflex which comes into play during walking and running. It causes an extension of the leg opposite from the flexed leg.

1.20 Intersegmental Reflexes are those reflex movements which involve more than one spinal segment.

1.21 Cooperative Reflex is so named because two or more reflexes aid or follow each other in a smooth pattern.

1.22 Competitive Reflexes involve either the inhibition of one reflex by another or one reflex being followed by an opposite reflex action. What occurs during competitive reflexes is that two or more stimuli are competing for a common neural pathway.

1.23 Successive Induction Reflex is the outcome of competing reflexes in which antagonistic reflexes follow each other in a definite pattern. An example of successive induction would be the two reflexes of flexion followed by extension which occur during walking or running.

1.24 Reflex Figure is a complex pattern involving the interactions of reflexes in all four limbs. The reflex figure is the basic coordinator of the walking and running movement. It integrates the alternating foot patterns and arm swings observable in walking.

1.30 Suprasegmental Reflexes are those reflexes which require participation of the brain centers, along with the pathways of the spinal cord and the muscles of the limbs and the trunk, for observable movement to occur.

1.31 Extensor Rigidity Reflex is a complex postural pattern primarily concerned with contraction of all the extensor or anti-gravity muscles of the arms and legs. Basically, it is viewed as an exaggerated extensor stretch reflex.

1.32 Plasticity Reactions bring about lengthening and shortening. The shortening reaction is a tendency for shortening to occur in an extensor muscle, and the lengthening response is just the reverse.

1.33 Postural Reflexes can be organized on a scale encompassing reflexes which cause little more than tonus (slight tensions) in certain body parts, to more tensions as an extensor rigidity, to even more specific complex postural adjustments such as placing and hopping reactions.

   1.331 Supporting Reactions are postural adjustments utilized by the body to maintain support in an upright position. Positive supporting reaction is the ubiquitous contraction of the flexor and extensor limb muscles causing a stiff rigid limb capable of maximum support. The negative supportive reaction is the relaxation of all the muscles of the limb.

   1.332 Shifting Reactions help the body remain supported under conditions of shifting weight. If a child is standing on the right leg with the left leg flexed and he begins to lose his balance in the direction of the flexed leg, a strong extensor tension will develop in the flexed limb to enable him to get the flexed leg to the ground, thus maintaining his balance.

1.333 Tonic-Attitudinal Reflexes create an increase in overall muscle tension. These reflexes are stimulated through kinesthetic influences in the neck which cause an adjustment of body posture corresponding to the position of the head, and through vestibular stimulation which also causes postural adjustments.

1.334 Righting Reactions help the individual regain balance. This reflex is stimulated by vestibular kinesthetic or visual modes.

1.335 Grasp Reflex is an involuntary grasping of any object placed in the palm of the hand. It is considered a posture reflex.

1.336 Placing and Hopping reactions are adjustments of the limbs to regain or establish a better base of support for the body. When an individual is thrown off balance in any direction he makes a series of little hops to reestablish his support limbs securely under him.

As has been stated previously, educators and curriculum developers need not concern themselves with writing behavioral objectives for this particular classification level. It is included in the taxonomy because it is the base upon which the learner builds his movement repertoire.

Classification Level Two—Basic-Fundamental Movements

Basic-fundamental movement patterns occur in the learner during his first year of life. He builds upon the reflex movements inherent within his body. The common basic movement behavior, such as visually tracking an object, reaching, grasping, and manipulating an object with the hands, and progressing through the developmental stages of crawling, creeping, and walking, emerge in the learner in a highly patterned and predictable way. All of these basic-fundamental movement patterns are built upon the foundation of reflex movements listed in the first classification level of this model. Many of these basic-fundamental movement patterns which develop early in the learner's life literally unfold from within rather than being taught.

The movements included in classification level 2.00, Basic-Fundamental Movements, are those inherent motor patterns which are based upon the reflex movements of the learner and which emerge without training. These movement patterns serve as the starting point for the further improvement of perceptual and physical abilities and are essential to the development of skilled movement.

Classification level two, Basic-Fundamental Movements, includes the following subcategories:

2.00 Basic-Fundamental Movements
   2.10 Locomotor Movements
   2.20 Non-Locomotor Movements
   2.30 Manipulative Movements
      2.31 Prehension
      2.32 Dexterity

2.00 Basic-Fundamental Movements are those inherent movement patterns which form the basis for specialized complex skilled movements.

   2.10 Locomotor Movements include those behaviors that change the stationary learner into an ambulatory learner. These kinds of movements bring about a change in location—getting the learner from one place to another. Included in this subcategory are the inherent movement behaviors of crawling, creeping, sliding, walking, running, jumping, hopping, rolling, and climbing.

   2.20 Non-Locomotor Movements include those movement behaviors which involve the limbs of the body or portions of the trunk in motion around an axis. The learner remains in one place and creates a dynamic movement pattern in space. Examples of non-locomotor movements are obvious when watching two children turn a rope for jump-rope activities or when observing one child utilizing both arms to turn his own rope. A basketball player uses non-locomotor movements when performing a free-throw and a ballet dancer uses non-locomotor arm movements with the corresponding basic foot positions. Behaviors included in this subcategory are pushing, pulling, swaying, stooping, stretching, bending, and twisting.

2.30 Manipulative Movements. Behaviors in this subcategory are usually described as coordinated movements of the extremities such as in piano playing, typing, or crayon work. These movements are usually combined with the visual modality, and in some instances with the tactile modality. This subcategory is concerned then primarily with movements of prehension and dexterity.

2.31 Prehension is the combining of several reflexes and the coordination of the visual perceptual abilities with prehensive activity. The component reflexes which join together to make up the prehensive movement are the flexion reflex, the gripping reflex, and the inhibitory reflex which causes the child to release the grasped object. With the combining of these three, a child, coordinating his abilities of visual discrimination with his manipulative abilities, can reach for and grasp a toy or block and voluntarily release his grip.

2.32 Dexterity of movement pertaining to the hand and fingers, implies a quick precise movement. This develops in the learner after he has mastered, to some extent, his prehensive movements, and acts as a basis for the development of skilled movements. At this level, manipulative movements include such activities as handling of blocks, cups, balls, and implements for drawing.

Once again, if the educator or curriculum developer is working with the "standard model" learner who has an efficiently functioning repertoire of basic-fundamental movements, behavioral objectives need not be written at this particular level in the taxonomy. However, if a learner is observed as having problems in this particular area, or if he is in a special program which is designed to provide him with activities to improve his basic-fundamental movements, then the writer should build for him a specialized curriculum stated in behavioral terms.

Cruickshank, et al.,[6] found that educators utilizing the "drainage theory" of physical activity with hyperactive children in an attempt to relax or settle them, were

[6]William M. Cruickshank, Frances A. Bentzen, Frederick H. Ratzeburg and Miriam T. Tannhauser, *A Teaching Method for Brain-Damaged and Hyperactive Children* (Syracuse: Syracuse University Press, 1961).

in reality obtaining the reverse effect. The expending of energies through vigorous physical activity appeared to make the hyperactive child more excitable. This type of child is more in need of experiences which help him to learn self-control and make him easier to manage in the classroom.

Obviously, then, the educator dealing with hyperactive children should challenge them with movement tasks which require concentrated effort and a minimum of distracting stimuli. A good example would be the skill of walking a balance beam. This skill could be used to help improve the child's balance and at the same time, hopefully, would enhance his ability to attend to a task. In the same manner, a novel manipulative skill could be utilized which would satisfy the educational goal established by the teacher as well as facilitate the development of an ever-increasing attention span in the hyperactive child. It should be remembered that not only must the activities selected for this type of child be stimulating and attention-getting, they must have intrinsic value and meet the identified movement and perceptual needs of these children.

The visually impaired learner has much the same needs for movement activities as does the sighted learner. However, because of his visual limitations, his participation in physical activity tends to be minimized, and this is detrimental to development, since many of the physical activities are essential to developing an efficiently functioning body. Investigators have noted that visually impaired learners demonstrate, among other movement inefficiencies, poor posture and faulty carriage. Therefore, a special set of behavioral objectives concerned with improving the basic-fundamental movements of the visually impaired students should be developed. The curriculum developer could construct a relevant movement program for the visually impaired learner based upon the behaviors which fall into this classification level and its corresponding subcategories. This particular classification level and the following one should prove most beneficial to educators who deal with the special child.

Classification Level Three—Perceptual Abilities

Though classification level three appears to suggest cognitive as well as psychomotor behaviors, it is included in the psychomotor domain because many investigators claim that perceptual and motor functions are inseparable, and enriched movement experiences usually enhance a child's abilities to structure and perceive more efficiently the many events to which he is exposed.

Efficiently functioning perceptual abilities are essential to development of the learner in the affective, the cognitive and the psychomotor domains. These abilities assist the learner in interpreting stimuli thus enabling him to make necessary adjustments to his environment. Present day society places high premiums on cognitive excellence and superior performance in psychomotor activities; both depend upon the development of perceptual abilities. It should be obvious that the learner should have maximum opportunities to engage early in sensory stimulating activities and opportunity to explore a variety of movement tasks to facilitate the development of these essential preceptual abilities.

Included in this third classification level, Perceptual Abilities, are the following subcategories and their corresponding divisions:

3.00 Perceptual Abilities
    3.10 Kinesthetic Discrimination
        3.11 Body Awareness
            3.111 Bilaterality
            3.112 Laterality
            3.113 Sidedness
            3.114 Balance
        3.12 Body Image
        3.13 Body Relationship to Surrounding Objects in Space
    3.20 Visual Discrimination
        3.21 Visual Acuity
        3.22 Visual Tracking
        3.23 Visual Memory
        3.24 Figure-Ground Differentiation
        3.25 Perceptual Consistency
    3.30 Auditory Discrimination
        3.31 Auditory Acuity
        3.32 Auditory Tracking
        3.33 Auditory Memory
    3.40 Tactile Discrimination
    3.50 Coordinated Abilities
        3.51 Eye-Hand Coordination
        3.52 Eye-Foot Coordination

3.00 Perceptual Abilities refer to all of the learner's perceptual modalities where stimuli impinge upon him to be carried to the higher brain centers for interpretation. In other words, data are provided which are then utilized by the brain centers when making a response decision. Of course, this all occurs in a fraction of a second.

3.10 Kinesthetic Discrimination encompasses accurate concepts of the body, body surfaces, and limbs. It also includes the right-left dimension and perceptual judgments of one's body in relation to surrounding objects in space, often referred to in the literature as spatial relationships. Behaviors which fall into this subcategory will deal primarily with the learner's awareness of his body and how it moves, his awareness of his position in space, and the relationship of his body to the surrounding environment. Kinesthesis, muscle sense, is a feeling sensation one gets when performing any movement pattern. It provides important feedback information for the learner thus enabling him to make necessary adjustments in his performance.

3.11 Body awareness is the *ability of the learner to recognize and control the body and body parts*. The learner becomes more aware of how his body functions when he is exposed to activities which stimulate his awareness of:

3.111 Bilaterality or movements performed by both sides of the body; catching a large playground ball illustrates this concept.

3.112 Laterality or movement performed by one side of the body or alternating from one side to another—ball bouncing utilizing one hand illustrates the laterality concept.

3.113 Sidedness or Dominance, in which the dominant side of the body takes the lead in an activity—when eating, writing or playing tennis the learner who has established dominance will always hold the implement in his dominant hand.

3.114 Balance. Though postural adjustments are actually reflex movements listed in classification level one, balance is included here because it is an important component of body awareness. Later, as the learner becomes involved in skilled movement and starts exploring changes in his base of support and his center of gravity he should have a working knowledge of body mechanics which deals with the application of the physical laws of motion upon the human body. This will supplement his postural reflexes and will facilitate the maintenance of his balance while performing a skilled movement. A child playing hopscotch is constantly changing his base of support and center of gravity when performing the movements involved in the game. For that matter, every living being constantly changes his base of support when walking. The hopscotch player must maintain his static (stationary) and dynamic (moving) balance without falling, throughout his performance, to be considered a successful player. When performing a one-leg balance, he changes his base of support from two feet to one; if he bends over while balancing on one leg and extends his trunk, head, and arms out in front of him and his opposite leg behind him, he has changed his center of gravity (concentration of weight) thereby making postural adjustments which will help him to maintain balance for an extended period of time. In a situation like the one just described, the reflex postural adjustments need assistance from the skilled performer. He must consciously do what he can to remain balanced.

3.12 Body Image is a concept which changes as the child matures. Its formation begins during the first few weeks of an infant's life and continues through adulthood. Children gain an awareness of their bodies when they first begin observable movements. The perception of one's body is important to the movement behaviors a child is capable of achieving. Cratty[7] suggests a developmental series which involves the child in activities designed to heighten his perception of his body. His definition appears to be all encompassing, covering the entire classification level of Kinesthetic Discrimination. For the purposes of this text, body image is operationally defined as the child's feelings regarding his body structure. Though this could logically

---

[7]Bryant J. Cratty, *Development Sequences of Perceptual-Motor Tasks: Movement Activities for Neurologically Handicapped and Retarded Children and Youth* (Long Island, New York: Educational Activities, 1967), p. 20.

be identified as belonging to the affective domain, the perception a child has concerning his body influences his movement achievements.

3.13 Body Relationship to Surrounding Objects in Space refers to the learner's directional concepts and awareness of his body and the design it creates in space.

3.20 Visual Discrimination, as a subcategory, is composed of five divisions, each one an important part of the total ability of discriminating visually.

3.21 Visual Acuity. According to Weymouth,[8] visual acuity encompasses an optical phase referred to as image production, a physiological phase which includes stimulation and neural interaction and neural conduction, and a perceptual phase occurring in the cortex. He defined visual acuity as the capacity to distinguish form and fine details. For the purposes of this text, visual acuity will be defined as the learner's ability to receive and differentiate between various observed objects, events and surroundings. Examples of behaviors which demonstrate that the

[8] Frank W. Weymouth, "Visual Acuity of Children," *Vision of Children: An Optometric Symposium*, eds., Monroe J. Hirsch and Ralph E. Wick (Philadelphia: Chilton, 1963), p. 119.

learner has developed visual acuity are his ability to distinguish between a circle and a square, between a "b" and a "d", and to select the small object from a group of objects of varying sizes.

3.22 Visual Tracking is the learner's ability to follow symbols or objects with coordinated eye movements. In order to read, the learner must develop this ability. The learner can be observed visually tracking when following the flight of an airplane or the flight of a ping pong ball. He visually tracks when he is picture-reading or when he is following the movements of a pendulum.

3.23 Visual Memory is much like auditory memory, the only difference being the stimulus reception or mode of entry. The learner demonstrates his ability to recall from memory past visual experiences when he is asked to draw from memory any of the geometric symbols, to write the alphabet or to spell a word. All of these examples presuppose the learner's ability to manipulate a writing instrument and to have cognizance of the figure names, the alphabet and word knowledge. Visual memory is also useful for recalling and performing previously observed movement patterns such as a sequence of steps in folk dance, a series of tumbling skills or a golf swing.

3.24 Figure-ground differentiation is the learner's ability to select the dominant figure from the surrounding background. Behaviors that indicate whether or not a learner has developed this perceptual ability are ball bouncing, ball catching, and any ball striking such as tennis and ping pong. In all of these activities the learner must be able to identify the dominant moving object and respond to it. Of course, all of the activities mentioned also include the degree of development the learner has achieved in eye-hand coordination.

3.25 Consistency refers to the learner's ability to be consistent in his interpretation when viewing the same type of object. In other words, even though coins are all different sizes, he should recognize that they can all be classified as round, thereby being consistent in his ability to recognize shapes and forms even though they have been modified in some way.

3.30 Auditory Discrimination is further analyzed into three divisions.

3.31 Auditory acuity is the learner's ability

to receive and differentiate between various sounds and their corresponding pitch and intensity. This division would include such behaviors as differentiating between the sounds of various instruments, identifying those sounds made by domestic animals, and selecting the correct vowel and consonant sounds from spoken words.

3.32 Auditory tracking refers to the learner's ability to distinguish the direction of the sound and to follow it.

3.33 Auditory memory is the learner's ability to recognize and reproduce post auditory experiences. Example behaviors would include repeating a nursery rhythm heard in school, playing from memory a song on the piano, repeating the pledge of allegiance to the flag, being able to introduce by name three people just introduced, and repeating the alphabet.

3.40 Tactile Discrimination is the learner's ability to differentiate between varying textures simply by using the tactile modality, *touching*. Tactile discrimination is exciting for the preschool learner to explore; he can understand more readily descriptive terms such as rough-smooth, hard-soft and sharp-dull if he can explore the concepts through tactile stimulation. This type of ability is essential to the visually impaired learner who must depend upon it to read Braille. It is beneficial to the young seamstress to be able to tactually differentiate between fabrics, and useful to the industrial arts student when determining the quality of his finish.

3.50 Coordinated Abilities incorporate activities which involve two or more of the perceptual abilities and movement patterns. This subcategory is primarily concerned with eye-hand and eye-foot coordinated abilities. The reader will note some overlap here. Behaviors which demonstrate that the learner has acquired the ability to coordinate two or more of the perceptual abilities are observable when the learner performs such activities as catching a ball or bean bag, hitting a tether-ball or tennis ball, bouncing a playground ball or kicking a moving soccer ball. These examples incorporate the ability to differentiate between the figure and the ground and to coordinate the visually perceived object with a manipulative movement of catching and a non-locomotor movement of kicking with the maintenance of balance while changing the base of support (lifting one leg from the ground). They also involve the child's ability to respond to a stimulus situation, often referred to as reaction or response time. This concept will be covered in classification level four.

3.51 Eye-Hand Coordination refers to the ability of the learner to select an object from its surrounding background and to coordinate the visually perceived object with a manipulative movement. In drawing or copying activities, the learner maintains constant visual control over the movement patterns of his hand. Eye-Hand Coordinated activities require visual accuracy and motor control.

3.52 Eye-Foot Coordination refers to the ability of the learner to differentiate an object from the surrounding background and to coordinate the visually perceived object with a movement of the lower limbs.

Though some of these perceptual abilities are not actually observable phenomena, the educator or curriculum developer will recognize whether or not the learner has developed any of the specific abilities by observing him in various movement and cognitive tasks. For example, ball bouncing is a combination of figure-ground differentiation and eye-hand coordination. If a learner is having difficulties with either of these two perceptual abilities it will be obvious. The educator would first investigate further the learner's ability to differentiate between the dominant figure and the surrounding background. If this is the learner's problem area, structured activities would be provided to minimize the difficulty, and behavioral objectives written with several ways stated for evaluating that particular perceptual ability.

Auditory discrimination is probably more related to cognitive behaviors even though when responding the learner uses a psychomotor act. For example, when a learner is requested to respond to directional commands by performing a psychomotor act such as facing a specific direction (the back wall), changing the level of his body posture (up-down), or moving in the requested direction (forward-backward), he is in fact demonstrating his understanding of spoken directional terms which is cognitive. His movements are primarily those that could be categorized in classification level two, Basic-Fundamental Movements. Nevertheless, the auditory discrimination abilities are included here because they need to be functioning efficiently to assist the learner in reaching his full potential in all the learning domains. So if a learner is found lacking in a high degree of development in any of the components of auditory discrimination, the educator can structure an auditory program written in behavioral terms for this particular learner, or the educator can write a structured auditory program in behavioral terms for a group of children.

The writing of behavioral objective statements begins at this classification level, unless of course, as previously mentioned, the educator is dealing with a learner who needs a structured program to improve his basic-fundamental movements. The subcategories and divisions listed in this *classification level could be utilized as an outline for a structured perceptual abilities program* (or, to recall a familiar term often found in the literature, perceptual motor program). *Once outlined the writer could develop behavioral objective statements for each subcategory and division in this part of the model. The behavioral objective statements could be written in order to evaluate the entire perceptual abilities program, one class in the program, or one learner in the class simply by modifying where necessary the evaluation component of the statement.*

The educator will be able to write behavioral objective statements for all the remaining classification levels if the movement behaviors unique to the established classifications are part of his curriculum.

Classification Level Four–Physical Abilities

Physical abilities are essential to the efficient functioning of the learner in the psychomotor domain. Proper functioning of the various systems of the body enable the learner to meet the demands placed upon him by his environment. These *physical abilities are in fact an essential part of the foundation for the development of skilled movements.*

This fourth classification level, Physical Abilities, incorporates the following characteristics which *if not adequately developed can be limiting factors to the development of highly skilled movement.*

4.00 Physical Abilities
    4.10 Endurance
        4.11 Muscular Endurance
        4.12 Cardiovascular Endurance
    4.20 Strength
    4.30 Flexibility
    4.40 Agility
        4.41 Change Direction
        4.42 Stops and Starts

4.43   Reaction-Response Time

4.44   Dexterity

4.00 Physical Abilities are those functional characteristics of organic vigor which when developed provide the learner with a sound, efficiently functioning instrument (his body) to be used when making skilled movements a part of his movement repertoire.

4.10 Endurance[9] is the ability of the body to supply and utilize oxygen enabling the learner to continue activity; it includes the body's ability to dispose of increased concentrations of lactic acid. When the learner goes through activities with the specific intent of improving his capacity to endure strenuous activity (training activities), he is in fact increasing the capillarization of muscle tissue. In other words, the difference between a trained and untrained learner is that the trained learner with a great capacity for endurance can work for longer periods of time and is more efficient in his movement patterns.

4.11 Muscular Endurance is the ability of a muscle or group of muscles to sustain for a long period of time.

4.12 Cardiovascular Endurance is the capacity of the learner to continue stren-

[9] Laurence E. Morehouse and Augustus T. Miller, *Physiology of Exercise* (St. Louis: C. V. Mosby Co., 1963), p. 237.

uous activity for periods of some duration. It includes the efficient interaction of the blood vessels, the heart, and the lungs. Like anything else there are degrees of cardiovascular endurance and the amount of this type of endurance varies with the specific task in which the learner is engaged. For example, for a preschool or primary child to play a game of run-and-tag takes a minimum cardiovascular endurance, when compared to the degree of cardiovascular efficiency (endurance) required of a cross-country runner. The level of development for this physical ability, cardiovascular endurance, should comply with or exceed the requirements of the task for efficient performance.

4.20 Strength as defined by Morehouse and Miller[10] is the learner's ability to "exert tension against resistance." Even though the degree of muscular strength a learner is capable of developing differs from learner to learner, it is developed only by exercising muscles against gradually increasing resistance. The learner can increase his muscular strength by exercising with weights, springs or by using his own body weight as he would in pull-ups or push-ups. To maintain the developed

---

[10] Morehouse and Miller, *Physiology of Exercise*, p. 59.

strength of a particular muscle, the learner must continually utilize that muscle. Lack of use of a muscle or muscle group decreases the size of the fibers within the muscle and increases the proportion of fat in the area. Strength is measured as the maximum amount of force exerted by a muscle or muscle group. Once again the level of development attained in this subcategory should correspond to the task required of the learner. If he is to chin himself, the level of arm muscle strength developed would not be as high a degree as would be required of a gymnast. Activities conducive to the development of arm strength, leg strength and abdominal strength would be included in this subcategory.

4.30 Flexibility is the range of motion in the joints that the learner is capable of achieving. A high degree of flexibility is needed to produce efficient movement and to minimize injury. Dance, gymnastics, and related areas are probably most concerned with flexibility activities.

4.40 Agility is the learner's ability to move quickly. It connotes dexterity and quickness of movement. The components of agility are rapid changes of direction, starting and stopping quickly, deftness of manipulative activities, and fast response times. A gymnast must have highly developed agility to efficiently

perform a free-exercise routine; a skilled vio-
linist must be dexterous to manipulate the
strings of his instrument; an elementary
school child must develop a certain degree of
agility to successfully participate in a dodgeball game, and a goal keeper in an ice hockey
game must have quick response time to efficiently perform his duties.

4.41 Change Direction refers to the learner's
ability to alter the direction in a movement without completely terminating
the activity.

4.42 Stops and Starts refer to the learner's
ability to initiate and terminate a
movement with a minimum of hesita-
tion. Efficient stopping and starting is
closely linked to response time.

4.43 Reaction-Response Time is essential to
motor performance. It can be defined
as the time that occurs between the
initiation of a stimulus and the initiation of the response.

4.44 Dexterity refers to the learner's deftness of manipulative activities. It refers
to fine motor skills involving precise
movements of the hand and fingers.

Coordination by itself is not included as a sub-category
because it is a component of skill mastery. When an
individual moves easily, with the sequence and timing of
his acts well controlled, he is described as being coor-

dinated. This essential element of motor performance is not readily measured objectively; however, high levels of achievement in any movement activity presupposes good coordination.

Though other disciplines will be concerned with this area, educators and curriculum developers in the areas of early childhood and physical education will be primarily concerned with writing behavior objectives for this classification level. The reader should note, however, that the physical abilities classification level is included in the taxonomy because of the important part these abilities play in efficient movement. The importance of each subcategory is dependent upon the specific task or motor skill to be performed by the learner. Therefore, the degree of skill attained is influenced not only by body build, acuity of the senses and reaction time, but also by endurance, strength, flexibility, and agility. Reaction time is important in efficient performance of many eye-hand and eye-foot coordinated tasks/skills in such activities as badminton, tennis and dodgeball. The development of flexibility plays an important role in the degree of skill attained by a student in dance, gymnastics or tumbling. The degree of endurance one develops could well determine who does or does not complete the Boston Marathon, and strength development must be commensurate with a performer's choice of activity if he has the desire to achieve high levels of success.

It is through the development of each learner's potential physical abilities that he will be better able to master the movements his body is capable of performing and attain his skill level. With the development of these attributes, the learner is in a better position to become a more efficient mover.

Classification Level Five—Skilled Movements

The term skill has been defined by several authors. Munn[11] defines skill as proficiency in performing a task; Laban and Lawrence[12] state that skill is the economy of effort a learner displays while perfecting a complex movement; they call skill the final state of perfection. Mohr[13] defines skill as a progress toward better performance; while Seashore[14] contends that skill is a degree of efficiency in performing a complex movement. Cratty[15] states that skill denotes that an integration of learner behavior regarding a specific task has occurred. In other words, he is calling skill a degree of efficiency in performance of a specific, reasonably complex movement behavior. The reader should note that all the authors appear to be selecting, in essence, the same unique characteristic, a degree of efficiency in performing a complex movement task. This classification level, skilled movement, will include movement tasks that require learning and are considered reasonably com-

[11] N. L. Munn, *Psychology* (Boston: Houghton Mifflin, 1946), p. 104.

[12] R. Laban and F. C. Lawrence, *Effort* (London: McDonald and Evans, 1947).

[13] Dorothy E. Mohr, "The Contributions of Physical Activity to Skill Learning," *American Association for Health, Physical Education and Recreation Research Quarterly*, vol. 31 (1960), p. 322.

[14] R. Seashore, "An Experimental and Theoretical Analysis of Fine Motor Skills," *American Journal of Psychology*, vol. 53 (1940), p. 86.

[15] Cratty, *Movement Behavior and Motor Learning*, p. 23.

plex. This will serve to distinguish between fundamental movements categorized in classification level 2.00, Basic-Fundamental Movement, and this classification level, 5.00, Skilled Movement.

Classification 5.00 deals with movement skills. The difference between a movement skill and a movement pattern should be obvious. A movement skill implies the development of a degree of proficiency or mastery. The movement pattern (fundamental movement) is the acceptable or recognizable performance of a movement for which the outcome alone is important.[16]

The classification level consists of two continuums, a vertical and a horizontal. The vertical continuum includes the degree of difficulty of the various movement skills to which learners are exposed. The continuum forms the basis for the hierarchical subcategories and is termed Levels of Complexity. The horizontal continuum deals with the levels of skill-mastery achieved by the learner; this continuum is called Levels of Proficiency. In other words, an educator will be able to categorize a movement behavior which falls into this classification level first by the degree of difficulty of the skill and second by the level of proficiency a learner achieves when performing the particular skill.

In classification level five, the corresponding subcategories, and the divisions are as follows:

5.00 Skilled Movements
5.10 Simple Adaptive Skill
5.11 Beginner

---

[16] Eugene Roach and Newell Kephart, *The Purdue Perceptual-Motor Survey* (Columbus, Ohio: Charles E. Merrill, 1966), p. 7.

                5.12 Intermediate
                5.13 Advanced
                5.14 Highly Skilled
     5.20 Compound Adaptive Skill
                5.21 Beginner
                5.22 Intermediate
                5.23 Advanced
                5.24 Highly Skilled
     5.30 Complex Adaptive Skill
                5.31 Beginner
                5.32 Intermediate
                5.33 Advanced
                5.34 Highly Skilled

5.00 Skilled Movement is the result of the acquisition of a degree of efficiency when performing a complex movement task. This classification level includes movements which require learning and are considered reasonably complex. Activities included in this classification level are those which involve some adaptation of the inherent movement patterns listed in classification level two, Basic-Fundamental Movements. All sports skills, dance skills, recreational skills, and manipulative skills fall into this classification. Some of the movement behaviors which will fall into this classification level will be difficult to distinguish from the movements categorized in classification level two, Basic-Fundamental Movements. A distinguishing feature is that in the classification level, Skilled Movement, the concern is with evaluating the learner's performance in terms of degree of proficiency or skill mastery attained. When dealing with movement behavior unique to the second classification level, the educator is concerned primarily with the development of certain perceptual abilities and evaluates the psychomotor behaviors in terms of whether or not a learner can perform, not how well he is performing.

The subcategories are not mutually exclusive and occasionally overlapping occurs. In like manner, it is difficult to draw a sharp dividing line on the horizontal continuum of skill-mastery. The extremes will always be obvious but the borderline cases may prove difficult to categorize. This is where precision in stating evaluation criteria plays a major role.

5.10 Simple Adaptive Skills, in most instances, refer to any adaptation of the movements in classification level two, Basic-Fundamental Movements. When basic movement patterns are changed or modified to suit the new situation or circumstance, they can be placed in this subcategory. In other words, almost any adaptation of an inherent movement pattern which requires some learning and is identified as being an important component of the curriculum could be classified as the first level of skilled movement. Example behaviors would include sawing a piece of wood, which is an adaptation of the push-pull movement or waltzing, which is an adaptation of the basic pattern of walking. Other movement behaviors within this subcategory include typing, clerical skills, piano playing, archery skills, skill in handicrafts, industrial skills, and other skills involving fine manipulative movements. Also included would be adaptation of such gross motor skills as hurdling, broad jumping or skating. Criteria for placing skilled movement behaviors into the subcategory are the limited extent of sensory information essential for completion of the task and the involvement of a portion of the performer's body. The rationale behind this subcategory is that once a learner has successfully performed the basic movement patterns and they have become efficient components of his movement vocabulary, it is relatively simple to learn an easy modification of these patterns. He becomes an efficient manager of his moving body and body parts.

5.11 Beginner

5.12 Intermediate

5.13 Advanced

5.14 Highly Skilled

5.20 Compound Adaptive Skill builds upon the learner's efficiencies in the basic skills and incorporates the management of an implement or tool. The learner now is expected to manage his body while utilizing an implement during the performance of a compound skill. Behaviors in this subcategory would include skills in all of the racket games such as tennis, badminton and ping pong. Hockey and golf would also be included. Needless to say, there will be some behaviors which will be difficult to categorize. Though this subcategory deals with activities that require the use of some instrument, educators will be able to identify activities that involve an implement but cannot logically be termed more complex than those activities found in the first subcategory. Perhaps an example will clarify the point. The activities of fencing, archery and canoeing all involve implements but the basic movement pattern is primarily a push-pull movement and a minimum of sensory information is needed to complete these tasks. Therefore the educator would logically place these kinds of activities into the first subcategory because they are in fact relatively simple adaptations of basic movement patterns. Earlier in the text it was noted that the subcategories are not mutually exclusive and some instances of overlap will occur.

5.21 Beginner

5.22 Intermediate

5.23 Advanced

5.24 Highly Skilled

5.30 Complex Adaptive Skills are skills which require greater mastery of the body mechanics—defined as the application of physical laws to the human body at rest or in motion.[17]   Examples of skilled movements which would be placed in this subcategory are aerial gymnastic stunts, difficult somersault or twisting dives and some of the more complicated trampoline stunts. Movements such as these, where the performer must judge space and estimate the time necessary to complete the skills are not easily mastered. Criteria for identifying a movement behavior which could be termed a complex skill are total bodily involvement of the performer, in many instances without a base of support, the necessity for making a series of delicate adjustments to sensations due to unexpected or uncontrolled cues, and the organization of movement within a larger space field.

5.31 Beginner

5.32 Intermediate

5.33 Advanced

5.34 Highly Skilled

The distinguishing features of the three subcategories are as follows. In the first subcategory the learner is attempting to manage his body efficiently in relation to the surrounding environment. In the second subcate-

[17]Movement Group Report, *Workshop Report: Purposeful Action* (Washington, D.C.: The National Association for Physical Education of College Women, 1956), p. 89.

gory another dimension is added. Now, in addition to efficiently managing his body, he becomes involved with the management of an instrument of some sort. The third subcategory becomes more complex for the learner. It requires total bodily involvement, in many instances without a base of support, and frequently occurring modifications of body posture due to unexpected or uncontrollable cues.

The following criteria may prove helpful when categorizing skilled movements into one of the three subcategories. The criteria for the first subcategory are the limited extent of sensory information essential for completion of the skill and the involvement of a portion of the performer's body or body parts. The criterion for the second subcategory is the extension of body parts through the use of an implement (e.g. racket, club, stick). The criteria for the third subcategory are total bodily involvement, in many instances without a base of support, the necessity of making postural adjustments due to unexpected cues and the organization of movement within a larger space field. It should be noted that while the subcategories are not mutually exclusive, they do provide a simple to complex continuum upon which all skilled movements can be placed. These subcategories may stimulate much discussion, nevertheless, they are offered as a simplified guide for categorizing skilled movement.

The rationale behind the selection of these three subcategories is obvious. Once the learner has developed his basic movement patterns, his perceptual abilities, and a certain amount of physical abilities, the next logical step is for him to modify his movement repertoire and develop skilled movements. At this level he develops a degree of efficiency in body management. The second level finds the learner involved with a racket or implement of some sort; now, he must learn to handle the implement in addition to managing his body during skilled movement. The third and final subcategory of this classification level finds the learner involved in intricate manipulations of his body during the performance of a skilled movement. Skills which fall into this subcategory are the most difficult to perform and master.

All skilled movement performed efficiently has a rhythm and beauty of its own. In the words of Xenophon:

> . . . what a disgrace it is for a man to grow old without ever seeing the beauty of which his body is capable.

Degree of Proficiency

A learner acquires skill by practicing and attending to the goal to be achieved. No matter where the learner is on the continuum of skill complexity, when he is introduced to a new skill he is a beginner in terms of the level of skill attained (degree of proficiency). It should be obvious that this other continuum exists within each subcategory. This continuum is termed degree of proficiency or skill mastery for that particular skill. In other words, a skill may be categorized as simple, such as a dance-walk, but the level of skill mastery between a beginning dancer and Martha Graham performing the same dance-walk is quite obvious. Even the difference between a highly skilled varsity football player and Joe Namath represents a difference in degree of proficiency or skill mastery.

The degree of proficiency (skill mastery) a learner is capable of achieving in a particular skilled movement can be divided into four levels; beginner, intermediate, advanced, and highly skilled. In reality the degree of proficiency represents a continuum of skill mastery, but these arbitrary divisions are provided to guide teachers in categorizing levels of mastery for any particular skill. Being able to recognize differences in the level of skill mastery achieved by learners provides important data for the educator in the selection of an effective teaching strategy. Jokl,[18] speaking on skilled movement and the individual stated,

> The untrained individual is restricted in respect to the effectiveness of the parts he is called upon to play, of diversity of the roles he can assume and thus of the inner attitudes he is able to adopt ... Since the neuromuscular system is our sole medium of communication, its differentiation through training represents a major determinant of the individual's power to act and react.

According to Jokl and other writers concerned with skilled movement, the nature and appearance of all levels of skilled movements are mediated through the motor areas of the central nervous system, and it is only through sustained practice that coordinative potentialities develop and the ability to convey cognitive qualities appears. Thus an individual attains a degree of proficiency or improves his performance of a practiced task by summating sensory data through the central ner-

[18]Ernest Jokl, "The Acquisition of Skill," *Quest VI: A Symposium on Motor Learning*, The National Association for Physical Education of College Women and the National College Physical Education Association for Men (May 1966), p. 25.

vous system, hopefully, leading to progressively effective motor responses. *The level of performance of a specific skill an individual can achieve is based upon the development of physical abilities, the development of the general supportive characteristics of the individual such as his levels of motivation and aspiration, and the development of various perceptual abilities.*

Jokl analyzed the acquisition of skill into four categories. The first category relates to the idea or concept of the task as imagined at the inception of the activity. The second category encompasses the learner's design of the skilled movement. The third category relates to the constructive plans aimed at organizing the task in appropriate sequence leading to completion of the activity, and the fourth category includes the motor technique utilized to attain the objective of the task. Though all of these components are essential to the acquisition of a specific task or skilled activity, they occur ordinarily with no awareness on the part of the individual.

He interpreted the first state or category as that of perception of the requirements of the whole task to be performed. He calls the acquisition of skill a prerequisite for the execution of purposive tasks. *It is through the acquisition of skill that one is able to extend the communication of the mind and the creation of aesthetic values.* Thus, when one can interpret the ideas or concepts of a specific task or, stated in simple terms, once the learner can place meaning to the task, he has taken the first step toward skill acquisition.

Using the background information from Jokl's article, it can be seen that becoming a skilled performer (mover) is like climbing a staircase to efficient performance of a skilled movement as shown in Figure 4. Each learner begins with the basic inherent movement patterns which form his foundation for movement skill learning. After imitation of the new movement pattern and initial trial and error learning, the learner should be able to perform the skill with some degree of confidence and similarity to the original movement; this would be considered a beginning skill level. With continued practice and heightened utilization of feedback from proprioceptors for adjustment purposes, the learner should be capable of performing the skill with an increased degree of movement efficiency. When he can, in fact, minimize the amount of extraneous motion, he could be categorized as being at the intermediate level of skill.

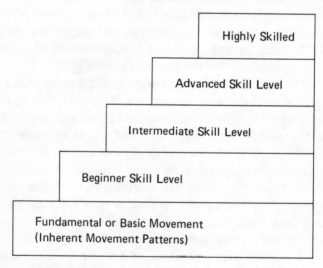

Figure 4—Degree of Proficiency—Level of Skill-Mastery

Once he becomes completely confident and can perform the skilled movement efficiently achieving almost the same response each time and his performance is superior in quality when compared to the performances of his peers, in other words, when he exceeds his peer-group expectancy, he can be categorized as functioning at the advanced skill level on the skill movement continuum. The learner becomes a professional performer when his vocation is based upon his ability to utilize his acquired skilled movements for the enjoyment of others.

To achieve high levels of success, the learner should be totally involved in any learning experience. However, the level of skill he attains might be affected by such physical factors as his body structure, his body function, the acuity of his sensory modalities and perceptual abilities.

There is an affective side to skill attainment. *The level of achievement in this category is definitely related to such affective factors as the learner's attitude toward achieving a high degree of efficiency in a skilled movement—his level of motivation and aspirations.* In other words, what value does the learner place upon acquisition of a high level of achievement in a particular skilled movement? Often, meaningful incentives or rewards, even if these have intrinsic value only, will facilitate progress in learning or improvement in the performance the learner is capable of attaining. Activities must be meaningful and worthwhile to the learner and in some way must match his system of values and interests. He must have an interest and the intent to achieve or learn a particular skilled movement or movement pattern. Of utmost importance is that the learner perceive the acquisition of this particular skill as being possible; he must be able to see success.

A learner's intent to learn any kind of skilled movement is usually more intense if it is based upon the intent to use the newly acquired skill for pursuits he categorizes as worthwhile. Means-end relationships are usually obvious. A student learns to type to facilitate work as a staff member of the school paper. A boy learns to work with engines so he can build himself a go-cart. A girl becomes interested in sewing so she can supplement her wardrobe. A youngster learns to play ball so he can make the Little League team. To reiterate, a learner converts opportunities into efficient learning when he recognizes the personal values of the particular skill.

Success in any skilled movement is determined by past learnings and experiences, efficient development in the two lower levels of this taxonomy, perceptual abilities, and physical abilities; it is also dependent upon intensive practice in the particular skill and also in a wide range of other skilled movement especially in early childhood, continuous motivation, and the meaningfulness of the activity to the learner.

Logically, there is a physiological limit beyond which the learner cannot go in speed, strength, endurance and accuracy of performance. Though this is a limiting factor to the level of skill development a learner is capable of achieving, few individuals have come close to approaching their limit.

The reader should note that many sports skills will

have a locomotor, a non-locomotor and in some instances a manipulative component. In a situation such as this, the learner may be evaluated on one component or on all components of the skilled movement.

Dividing the movement into component parts not only allows for a more accurate evaluation, but provides the learner with more specific details which he can utilize when making movement corrections. Movements are divided into component parts for the highly skilled performer only because he is at a stage of learning a particular skill or skills at which he can benefit from the detailed analysis. The learner who is performing at the beginner skill level becomes confused with too much analysis of inefficient movements. The learner performing at the intermediate skill level begins to do some self-analysis of movement errors, but once again does not benefit from too much detail.

It is possible for the educator who deals primarily with movement skills to divide his curriculum into major units and to utilize this classification level to categorize all the essential movement behaviors into appropriate categories. Once he has organized his program into units and has identified the specific skills within each unit, constructing behavioral objective statements for each corresponding skill becomes a manageable task and facilitates relevant evaluations. It must, however, be remembered that evaluating performance cannot be considered absolute or precise measurement. Evaluation must always be carried on in light of the goals for which the teaching strategies were planned and with the realization that some uncertainty and chance error are always present.

After developing some proficiencies in the performance of skilled movement, the learner is better equipped to explore the realm of Non-Discursive Communication.

Classification Level Six—
Non-Discursive Communication

Movement communication is obvious in everyday life and is an important aspect of the learner's movement behaviors. Each learner develops a style of moving which communicates his feelings about his affective self to the perceptive observer. Accurately interpreting communicative movement behaviors of a learner heightens an educator's perceptions of the learner's feelings, needs, and interest, thereby enabling the educator to make more meaningful selections of learning strategies for that particular learner.

Behaviors that fall into this classification level are both innate and learned. The innate movement communications are those observed in the learner during his first few months of life and are created by combining reflexes; they are not considered voluntary purposeful movements. These innate movement communications are types of emotional expression; the crying response or fear response of a young learner are lucid illustrations. The learned behaviors of movement communication are those predominantly composed of movements which are performed to convey a message to the receiver. Waving to an approaching friend needs no interpretation; it is almost the universal symbol or communicative movement which means hello; in like manner, waving to a departing friend means good-bye. Movement communication is accurately termed Non-Discursive Communication. The terminology removes from this classification level the movements of speech production. Actually, the movements utilized to produce sound are inherent within the "normal" learner; these kinds of movement would never go beyond classification level two, Basic-Fundamental Movements. Any improvements the learner makes in speech are in reality improvements in his command of the verbal language and increased comprehension of the techniques of projection and presentation, and therefore, would more accurately be labeled cognitive improvements.

> 6.00 Non-Discursive Communication
> > 6.10 Expressive Movement
> > > 6.11 Posture and Carriage
> > > 6.12 Gestures
> > > 6.13 Facial Expression
> > 6.20 Interpretive Movement
> > > 6.21 Aesthetic Movement
> > > 6.22 Creative Movement

6.00 Non-Discursive Communication is the classification level composed of behaviors which can be labeled forms of movement communication. These forms of movement behavior *encompass a wide variety of communicative movements ranging from facial expressions, postures, and gestures to sophisticated modern dance choreographies.* Many of the studies concerned with movement communication are based upon the assumption that the better an individual can assess and utilize movement communications transmitted by a second individual the better will be the interpersonal relationships between the two.

6.10 Expressive Movement is composed of communicative movements used in everyday life. It has three components, body posture and carriage, gestures, and facial expressions. These types of movement are overt bodily expressions which communicate the learner's internal emotional state and which accompany his verbal communication to place more emphasis upon his words. They are the unspoken language of friendship, sympathy and love. The communicative movements of gestures, body posture and carriage, and facial expressions are a form of sign language which the child learns to interpret and use early in life. Though each learner has his own characteristic movement expressions, the more common ones are universally recognizable. There are movement expressions, however, which are unique to a particular culture. Since movement expression in many instances is not part of the formal curriculum, educators need not be concerned about writing behavioral objectives for movement behaviors which fall into this particular subcategory. They are included in the taxonomy because movement expressions are modified, exaggerated and utilized by learners in the fine arts area who are performing movement interpretations.

6.11 Posture and Carriage

6.12 Gestures

6.13 Facial Expressions

6.20 Interpretive Movement is composed of aesthetic movement and creative movement. These represent the highest level of movement development. Aesthetic and creative movements are considered art forms. Langer[19] states that works of art do what language cannot readily do. Works of art are capable of presenting for the viewer the nature and patterns of sensitive and emotional life; they are in reality expressive forms which relate to human feelings. Movement works of art are the performer's means of giving an objective symbol (the design his body makes in space by the execution of a movement) to subjective events (inner feelings and emotions). Interpretive movement is the expression of a skilled performer's knowledge of many human feelings and of the most efficient utilization of the body.

6.21 Aesthetic movements are those skilled movements which are performed efficiently by the learner, creating for the

[19] Susanne K. Langer, *Problems of Art* (New York: Charles Scribner's Sons, 1957), pp. 8–21.

viewer an image of effortless beautiful motion. All the sports skills executed by learners who have reached a high degree of skill in the performance of any movement could be classified as aesthetic movement.

6.22 Creative movements are those movements performed to communicate to the viewer some message or just to be observed as a dynamic design cut in space. Once again the performer must be a highly skilled mover with a knowledge of body mechanics and must have highly developed physical and perceptual abilities. Performers executing movements in this subcategory build upon the Movement Expressions, thereby assisting the viewer in his interpretation of the dynamic movement design.

Educators who deal with the highest levels of movement development will be more concerned with this classification level than will other educators. This does not mean, however, that preschool and elementary children are not to explore movement behaviors in Non-Discursive Communication.

Young learners already possess movement behaviors unique to the subcategory of Expressive Movement, and can interpret these kinds of Non-Discursive Communications when transmitted by another. How often have young learners been heard to say "Teacher is mad today!" or "She looks tired." These kinds of verbal comments are based upon the viewer's observation of another person's expressive movements. The young learner must also be allowed to explore the realm of Interpretive Movement expressing his feelings and emotions through movement behaviors in his curriculum. Children need the experiences of utilizing their bodies to perform interpretive movement.

An example of a behavioral objective written for the subcategory of interpretive movement may help to clarify the point:

> *To increase in kindergarten children their abilities to utilize and explore interpretive movements so that when given the opportunity in a class situation to explore interpretive movements to music each child will respond by performing locomotor and non-locomotor movements.*

Young learners who are not highly skilled movers will not be able to reach the same degree of proficiency in interpretive movements as would the skilled athlete or skilled dancer, and therefore would be evaluated differently.

To construct behavioral objectives for classification level six, Non-Discursive Communication, the writer must first be able to specify his intended goals and categorize the learner's movement behaviors.

The reader should remember that in order for a learner to reach the highest level of achievement in movement behaviors he must begin with efficiently functioning reflex mechanisms and inherent movement patterns, must improve perceptual and physical abilities, and must become a skilled mover building upon this foundation the ability to communicate non-discursively.

Summary Outline of Psychomotor Taxonomy

The complete model with its classification levels, subcategories and divisions for classifying movement behaviors unique to the psychomotor domain is as follows:

    1.00   Reflex Movements
          1.10   Segmental Reflexes
                 1.11   Flexion Reflex
                 1.12   Myotatic Reflex
                 1.13   Extensor Reflex
                 1.14   Crossed Extensor Reactions
          1.20   Intersegmental Reflexes
                 1.21   Cooperative Reflex
                 1.22   Competitive Reflex
                 1.23   Successive Induction
                 1.24   Reflex Figure
          1.30   Suprasegmental Reflexes
                 1.31   Extensor Rigidity
                 1.32   Plasticity Reactions
                 1.33   Postural Reflexes
                        1.331   Supporting Reactions
                        1.332   Shifting Reactions
                        1.333   Tonic-Attitudinal Reflexes
                      1.334   Righting Reaction
                        1.335   Grasp Reflex
                      1.336   Placing and Hopping Reactions
    2.00   Basic-Fundamental Movements
          2.10   Locomotor Movements
          2.20   Non-Locomotor Movements
          2.30   Manipulative Movements
                 2.31   Prehension
                 2.32   Dexterity

3.00 Perceptual Abilities
   3.10 Kinesthetic Discrimination
      3.11 Body Awareness
         3.111 Bilaterality
         3.112 Laterality
         3.113 Sidedness
         3.114 Balance
      3.12 Body Image
      3.13 Body Relationship to Surrounding Objects in Space
   3.20 Visual Discrimination
      3.21 Visual Acuity
      3.22 Visual Tracking
      3.23 Visual Memory
      3.24 Figure-Ground Differentiation
      3.25 Perceptual Consistency
   3.30 Auditory Discrimination
      3.31 Auditory Acuity
      3.32 Auditory Tracking
      3.33 Auditory Memory
   3.40 Tactile Discrimination
   3.50 Coordinated Abilities
      3.51 Eye-Hand Coordination
      3.52 Eye-Foot Coordination

4.00 Physical Abilities
   4.10 Endurance
      4.11 Muscular Endurance
      4.12 Cardiovascular Endurance
   4.20 Strength
   4.30 Flexibility
   4.40 Agility
      4.41 Change Direction
      4.42 Stops and Starts

It should be recognized that any classification model is merely an attempt to abstract and classify learner behaviors to facilitate the organization of meaningful content within the curriculum and to structure relevant evaluations of the outcomes of learning. When behavioral objectives writers and curriculum developers are able to classify educational objectives into one of the three domains and further clarify learner behaviors into a specific category within a domain, the teaching strategies become more apparent, thus giving meaningful directions for desired learner outcomes.

This taxonomic model is offered as a way of viewing, explaining, and categorizing the components of the psychomotor domain. It is in no way a rigidly fixed conceptual model, but a flexible model capable of shrinking or expanding as experience, new ideas, and critical reviewers dictate its adaptation. This is an effort to categorize the movement experiences of the learner. It is a logical classification of movement experiences and is consistent with accepted theories and principles of motor learning. Though many statements and concepts from different models and movement theories are apparent within this model, it is not intended as a synthesis of all works, but rather as a hierarchy of learning in the psychomotor domain. It has been developed to help behavioral objective writers and curriculum developers classify student learning experiences and define objectives as meaningful descriptions of student behaviors.

CHAPTER IV

Utilizing the Psychomotor Domain When Writing Behavioral Objectives

SPECIAL CONSIDERATIONS

There is a definite need for an understanding of a learner's movement behavior in the psychomotor domain. Though it is obvious that aspects of learner behaviors can logically be placed in any of the three learning domains, the educator must focus upon the primary concern of the goal statement. Most behaviors are combinations of the cognitive, the affective, and the psychomotor and though impossible to categorize exclusively as being only one of the three, the educator when writing behavioral objectives for a particular learner or group of learners must focus upon the primary purpose or intent of the objective and organize the evaluation to reflect a real difference in the learner's behavior. There will be instances when the goal statement is cognitive and the learner performs a psychomotor act to demonstrate his cognition. The educator will, however, be evaluating the cognitive aspects of the learner's behavior; handwriting will serve as an excellent illustration of this concept. Handwriting is a psychomotor act and often a learner performs a handwriting task during a test situation; perhaps he is requested to write an essay. Usually if he is in the upper intermediate grades or higher, the teacher will grade primarily on content and grammar; the objective would therefore be logically categorized as cognitive. If the teacher decides that his penmanship is in need of improvement, he may also grade the learner's handwriting. On this grading, the content and grammar are disregarded and only letter formation comes under attention. Now the teacher has an objective that is both cognitive and psychomotor and is logically evaluating both aspects of a learner's particular behavior. As long as the teacher recognizes the aspects of a particular learner behavior and adequately evaluates the behavior from each domain, being sure to use appropriate methods and reasonable criteria, he is on the right track.

Using the scheme outlined in the previous chapter, the movement behaviors of a curriculum can be analyzed and the relevant behaviors can be categorized into a classification level of the taxonomy for the psychomotor domain. However, there will be movements that can logically be categorized in several different levels, like the rope jumping activity which is obviously dependent upon a basic movement—jumping—and perceptual abilities; eye-foot coordination, and body awareness. Once modified to incorporate various stunts, rope jumping can easily be categorized as a skilled movement. Therefore, it becomes the task of the educator to determine the primary goal, classify the activity accordingly and write the behavioral statement, utilizing an appropriate evaluating instrument or learner performance along with reasonable criteria. In those instances where meaningful criteria are difficult to state, as in creative movements of preschool children, the peer-group expectancy model is useful and provides the educator with a means of trying to objectively evaluate the movement behaviors of learners.

Since a behavioral objectives statement developed through the goals-approach is formalized through the construction of two explicitly stated major components, it follows that the completed statement should convey the exact intended goal and evaluation methodology of the writer. Since little, necessarily, must be left for interpretation, the exact intention of the behavioral objective must be stated—the goal statement, the exact learner's performance or measuring instrument must be identified—the first part of the evaluation statement, and the level of achievement required of the learner along with a statement of teacher-expectancy, if the behavioral objective is written to evaluate the progress of a group—the second part of the evaluation statement.

The examples utilized in this text are provided as guides. The author does not intend to suggest they are perfect examples of behaviorally stated objectives; they are provided in an effort to give the educator a clear understanding of how to go about developing behavioral objectives after categorizing the relevant movement behaviors essential for achievement in their particular curriculum. The evaluations for each stated goal are provided to stimulate the innovative educator into developing several pupil performance requirements which will adequately measure the desired outcome of each child's movement learning.

Perhaps a simplified chart would be most beneficial to reinforce for the reader the concepts of the previous chapter. Figure 5 illustrates a simplification of the taxonomy continuum subcategories and their corresponding classification levels. Each classification level is followed by a brief definition, and a few sample behavioral activities to further clarify for the reader the kinds of movement behavior which most logically are placed within each level.

With the classification levels and examples of their characteristic movement behaviors the following samples of behavioral objective statements, organized by classification level and subcategory, illustrate the utilization of this taxonomy when structuring a movement curriculum in behavioral terms.

1.00 Reflex Movements

As has previously been stated, the behavioral objective writer need not concern himself with writing objectives for the first classification level of this taxonomy. This first classification, Reflex Movements, was included in the taxonomy because of its importance to movement behaviors.

2.00 Basic-Fundamental Movements

The second classification level, Basic-Fundamental Movement, is composed of locomotor, non-locomotor, and manipulative movements which are, in fact, several reflexes combined into predetermined patterns. If the educator is designing a movement curriculum in behavioral terms for the "normal" learner he probably will do little more than utilize the movements in this classifi-

Figure 5—Taxonomy for the Psychomotor Domain: Classification Levels and Subcategories

Taxonomy Continuum	Levels	Definitions	Behavioral Activity
1.10 Segmental 1.20 Inter-segmental 1.30 Supra-segmental	1.00 Reflex Movements	Actions elicited without conscious volition in response to some stimuli	Flexion, extension, stretch, postural adjustments
2.10 Locomotor 2.20 Non-Locomotor 2.30 Manipulative	2.00 Basic-Fundamental Movements	Required: 1.00 Inherent movement patterns which are formed from a combining of reflex movements, and are the basis for complex skilled movement	2.10 Walking, running, jumping, sliding, hopping, rolling, climbing 2.20 pushing, pulling, swaying, swinging, stooping, stretching, bending, twisting 2.30 handling, manipulating, gripping, grasping finger movements
3.10 Kinesthetic Discrimination	3.00 Perceptual Abilities	Required: 1.00–2.00 Interpretation of stimuli from various modalities provid-	The *outcomes* of perceptual abilities are observable in *all purposeful* movement.

		Examples:
	ing data for the learner to make adjustments to his environment	
3.20	Visual Discrimination	Auditory— following verbal instructions.
3.30	Auditory Discrimination	Visual—dodging a moving ball.
3.40	Tactile Discrimination	Kinesthetic— making bodily adjustments in a hand-stand to maintain balance.
3.50	Coordinated Abilities	Tactile—determining texture through touch. Coordinated—jump rope, punting, catching.
4.00	Physical Abilities	Functional characteristics of organic vigor which are essential to the development of highly skilled movement
4.10	Endurance	All activities which require strenuous effort for long periods of time—Examples: distance running, distance swimming.
4.20	Strength	All activities which require muscular exertion—Examples: weight lifting, wrestling.
4.30	Flexibility	All activities which require wide range of motion at hip joints—Examples: touching toes, back bend, ballet exercises.

Taxonomy Continuum	Levels	Definitions	Behavioral Activity
4.40 Agility			All activities which require quick precise movements—Examples: shuttle run, typing, dodgeball.
5.10 Simple Adaptive Skill	5.00 Skilled Movements	A degree of efficiency when performing complex movement tasks which are based upon inherent movement patterns	All skilled activities which build upon the inherent locomotor and manipulative movement patterns of classification level two.
5.20 Compound Adaptive Skill			
5.30 Complex Adaptive Skill			These activities are obvious in sports, recreation, dance, and fine arts areas.
6.10 Expressive Movement	6.00 Non-discursive Communication	Communication through bodily movements ranging from facial expressions through sophisticated choreographies	Body postures, gestures, facial expressions, all efficiently executed skilled dance movements and choreographies.
6.20 Inter-pretive Movement			

Figure 5 (*Continued*)

cation level as a means for sophisticating the perceptual abilities, improving the physical abilities, establishing a foundation for skilled movement and as a vehicle for initial experiences of creative movement. However, the educator dealing with learners needing additional stimulating experiences to strengthen these movement activities, will write behavioral objectives for the specifically identified movement behavior needs of the learner.

Examples of objectives written in the Basic-Fundamental movement categories are:

2.00 Basic-Fundamental Movements

To improve the fundamental patterns of preschool children so that by the end of the year each child will be able to perform satisfactorily all locomotor, non-locomotor and manipulative movements within the normal range of his peer-group as determined through subjective teacher analysis.

Critique:

Goal—To improve the fundamental movement patterns of preschool children.

Evaluation—So that by the end of the year each child will be able to perform the locomotor, non-locomotor and manipulative movements within the normal range of his peer-group as determined through subjective teacher analysis.

Behavioral Activity—Be able to perform the locomotor, non-locomotor, and manipulative movements.

Success Level—

  (a) Teacher Expectancy—Each child
  (b) Learner Requirement—Within the normal range of his peer-group as determined through subjective teacher analysis.

This particular objective is written to evaluate the progress of an entire group of preschool children. However, by changing the identified learner group, the objective could be used to evaluate the progress of one special child. The modified objective would read as follows:

> To improve the fundamental movement patterns of *Tom Jones* so that by the end of the year *he* will be able to satisfactorily perform the locomotor, non-locomotor, and manipulative movements within the normal range of his peer-group.

It should be further noted that as criteria, the group or individual learner's performances are actually being compared to expected kinds of movement behaviors characteristic of the identified learner's developmental level.

2.10 Locomotor Movements

Locomotor movements include those behaviors which transport the learner from one location to another. The inherent movement patterns of walking, running, jumping, hopping, rolling and climbing are included here.

The following are illustrations of behavioral objective statements. The first example purports to evaluate several locomotor movements performed by an identified group of special education children. The next two examples are each measuring specific locomotor movement behaviors. From these examples it should be obvious to the reader that he may group several behaviors into one statement or he may develop his behavioral objective statement to measure just one particular behavior.

2.10 Locomotor Movements

A. To improve in the special education children the basic locomotor movements so that each child will be able to perform the following activities: sliding, walking, running, jumping with smooth movement patterns and gait so they do not deviate significantly from the mean performances of their peer-group.

Critique:

Goal—To improve in the special education children the basic locomotor movement.

Evaluation—So that each child will be able to perform the following activities: sliding, walking, running, jumping with smooth movement patterns and gait.

Behavioral Activity—Will be able to perform sliding, walking, running, jumping.

Success Level—
  (a) Teacher Expectancy—Each child
  (b) Learner Requirement—With smooth movement patterns and gait so they do not deviate significantly from the mean performances of their peer-group.

B. To improve in preschool children the fundamental locomotor movement of executing a two-footed jump so that by the end of the year one hundred percent of the children will be able to jump forward starting with both feet parallel, using the arms properly for forward thrust and landing with both feet together.

Critique:

Goal—To improve in preschool children the fundamental locomotor movement of executing a two-footed jump.

Evaluation—So that by the end of the year one hundred percent of the children will be able to jump forward starting with both feet parallel, using the arms properly for forward thrust and landing with both feet together.

Behavioral Activity—To jump forward.

Success Level—

(a) Teacher Expectancy—One hundred percent of the children.
(b) Learner Requirement—Starting with both feet parallel, using the arms properly for forward thrust and landing with both feet together.[1]

C. To improve in preschool children the abilities of ascending and descending stairs so that when given the opportunity to walk up and down a flight of twenty stairs each child will be able to do so correctly, utilizing an alternating foot pattern.

Critique:

Goal—To improve in preschool children the abilities of ascending and descending stairs.

Evaluation—So that when given the opportunity to walk up and down a flight of twenty stairs each child will be able to do so, correctly utilizing an alternating foot pattern.

Behavioral Activity—Walk up and down a flight of twenty stairs.

Success Level—

(a) Teacher Expectancy—Each child
(b) Learner Requirement—Correctly utilizing an alternating foot pattern.

[1] The explicitly stated criteria provide for the evaluator specific movement patterns to observe when judging the degree of success attained by the learner.

2.20 Non-Locomotor Movements

Non-Locomotor Movements include behaviors which involve pushing, pulling, swaying, stooping, stretching, bending and twisting. This type of movement behavior is characterized by motion around the body axis which involves the limbs of the body or portions of the trunk.

2.20 Non-Locomotor Movements

To improve the basic throwing pattern of preschool children so that by the end of the year each child is able to perform an overarm throw, stepping forward with the opposite leg, shifting his body weight, using his arm at a slight angle from his shoulder and releasing, thus enabling the ball to travel at least six feet.

Critique:

Goal—To improve the basic throwing pattern of pre-school children.

Evaluation—So that by the end of the year each child is able to perform an overarm throw, stepping forward with the opposite leg, shifting his body weight, using his arm at a slight angle from his shoulder and releasing thus enabling the ball to travel at least six feet.

Behavioral Activity—To perform an overarm throw.

Success Level—

    (a) Teacher Expectancy—Each child

    (b) Learner Requirement—Stepping forward with the opposite leg, shifting his body weight, using his arm at a slight angle from his shoulder, and releasing thus enabling the ball to travel at least six feet.[2]

---

[2] The learner requirement looks formidable, but in reality is quite simple. Each part of the requirement is easily observable to the eye or can be accurately measured.

2.30 Manipulative Movements

These movements are performed predominantly by the hand and fingers. They are movements of prehension which involve grasping or gripping implements or objects and releasing, and movements characterized by dexterity. Behaviors unique to this subcategory are coloring, ball handling, block building and tool manipulation.

2.30 Manipulative Movements

For preschool children to improve their dexterity in manipulating their hands and fingers so that given a shoe string and a play shoe, ninety percent of the children can decrease by two seconds the time necessary to lace and tie the shoe on a before-and-after test.

Critique:

Goal—For preschool children to improve their dexterity in manipulating their hands and fingers.

Evaluation—So that given a shoe string and a play shoe, ninety percent of the children can decrease by two seconds the time necessary to lace and tie the shoe on a before-and-after test.

Behavioral Activity—To lace and tie the shoe.

Success Level—

    (a) Teacher Expectancy—Ninety percent of the children.

    (b) Learner Requirement—To show on a before-and-after test a time decrease of two seconds.

2.31 Prehension

To improve in preschool children the ability to manipulate drawing implements, blocks, and balls, so that by the end of the year each child will satisfactorily handle crayons, paint brushes, and chalk without deviating significantly from the norm of his peer-group; can construct block towers at least five blocks high; and can roll accurately a large ball to a friend, can catch a rolling ball each time without missing, and can bounce-pass a large ball to a friend accurately.

Critique:

Goal—To improve in preschool children the ability to manipulate drawing implements, blocks, and balls.

Evaluation—So that by the end of the year each child will satisfactorily handle crayons, paint brushes, and chalk without deviating significantly from the norm of his peer group; can construct block towers at least five blocks high; and can roll accurately a large ball to a friend, can catch a rolling ball each time without missing, and can bounce-pass a large ball to a friend accurately.

Behavioral Activity—Will handle crayons, paint brushes and chalk, can construct block towers, can roll a large ball, catch a rolling ball and bounce-pass a large ball.

Success Level—
  (a) Teacher Expectancy—Each student.
  (b) Learner Requirement—Without deviating significantly from the norm of his peer-group can build at least five blocks high, accurately roll, catch without missing, accurately bounce-pass.

2.32 *Dexterity*

To improve manual dexterity in preschool children so that by the end of the year ninety-five percent of the children can correctly button and zip their own clothing and put their shoes on the proper feet and tie them without making knots.

Critique:

Goal—To improve in preschool children manual dexterity.

Evaluation—So that by the end of the year ninety-five percent of the children can correctly button and zip their own clothing and put their shoes on the proper feet and tie them without making knots.

Behavior Activity—Button and zip clothing, put on their own shoes, and tie their own shoes.

Success Level—

(a) Teacher Expectancy—Ninety-five percent of the children.

(b) Learner Requirement—Correctly button and zip their own clothing, put their shoes on the proper feet and tie them without making knots.

Occasionally it is difficult to state meaningful criteria for some activities which fall into this classification level, Basic-Fundamental Movements. Individual posture and body-carriage differ for learners while standing or moving and this makes the selection of rigid criteria difficult and perhaps at times unfair. It should be apparent, because of varying body structures, that learners cannot all be forced into the same rigid postural mold.

Educators are constantly evaluating a learner's behaviors through unobstrusive observations, and usually the behaviors that deviate from the group are those that are quickly identified. Because this is often the practice, the peer-group expectancy model proves most beneficial at this point. If the learner's fundamental movement behaviors are comparable to what is considered normal for his peer-group, he can be classified as progressing satisfactorily.

3.00 Perceptual Abilities

The refinement of a learner's perceptual abilities usually becomes the responsibility of the early childhood educators. Since these abilities are actually prerequisites to learning in all the domains it seems only natural that they become the prime concern of educators who guide learners through their first experiences with formal education.

This classification level also should prove most beneficial to the educator involved in a perceptual-motor program. If the movement behaviors unique to this type of program are *first organized* into their corresponding subcategories and are further classified by division within the subcategory, the writer will have an outline from which to construct his behavioral objective statements.

Probably the easiest way to proceed is to utilize the specific terms assigned to each division as the behavior the educator desires to improve or develop. Of course when using the goals-approach this particular behavior is called the learning task. When the educator has the list of movement behaviors under each division, these can be used as performances the learner demonstrates to measure the success attained for that particular behavioral objective. The writer needs only to provide the desired level of success the learner must achieve and the teacher expectancy, if evaluating the entire class on their achievement in a particular perceptual ability, and the behavioral objective statement is complete.

Since perceptual abilities are so essential for further development, it is more beneficial to view the progress of each individual learner as opposed to group progress. The additional information provided by the teacher-expectancy can be utilized by the educator to make decisions regarding the effectiveness of his teaching strategies.

The reader will note that the preceding examples follow, for the most part, the subcategories or their corresponding divisions in the Perceptual Abilities classification level.

3.10 Kinesthetic Discrimination

A. To improve body balance in preschool children so that when given the opportunity to perform on the balance beam ninety percent of the children can walk forward and backward the length of the beam without falling and seventy-five percent of the children can maintain balance on one leg for at least one second.

Critique:

Goal—To improve body balance in preschool children.

Evaluation—So that when given the opportunity to perform on the balance beam ninety percent can walk forward and backward the length of the beam without falling and seventy-five percent can maintain balance on one leg for at least one second.

Behavioral Activity—Can walk forward and backward the length of the beam and can maintain balance on one leg.

Success Level—

  (a) Teacher Expectancy—Ninety percent and seventy-five percent.

  (b) Learner Requirement—The length of the beam without falling and can maintain balance for at least one second.

B. To develop in preschool children an awareness of their bodies so that by the end of the year each child will be able to point to the correct body part upon verbal command and will be able to demonstrate at least one movement for each body part.

Critique:

Goal—To develop in preschool children an awareness of their bodies.

Evaluation—So that by the end of the year each child will be able to point to the correct body part upon verbal command and will be able to demonstrate at least one movement for each body part.

Behavioral Activity—To point to the body part and to demonstrate movement for each body part.

Success Level—

  (a) Teacher Expectancy—Each child.

  (b) Learner Requirement—The correct body part and at least one movement.

3.20 Visual Discrimination

To develop in preschool children the abilities of visual acuity as determined by each child's ability to correctly categorize by shape a group of ten building blocks making no more than two errors.

Critique:

Goal—To develop in preschool children the abilities of visual acuity.

Evaluation—As determined by each child's ability to correctly categorize by shape a group of ten building blocks making no more than two errors.

Behavioral Activity—Categorize by shape a group of ten building blocks.

Success Level—

  (a) Teacher Expectancy—Each child
  (b) Learner Requirement—Making no more than two errors.[3]

3.22 Visual Tracking

To improve in preschool children the ability to visually track a moving object so that when participating in a fast moving circle game of ball rolling each child will be able to keep track of the moving ball and when it is rolled to him he will be able to catch it without missing.

Critique:

Goal—To improve in preschool children the ability to visually track a moving object.

Evaluation—So that when participating in a fast moving circle game of ball rolling each child will be able to

---

[3] It is obvious that the learner is also using the manipulative movement, prehension, as he places each block in its proper place. Nevertheless, the prime concern of the educator at the time must have been the learner's visual acuity (cognitive recognition of shapes) and so that is the variable which has been isolated for evaluation.

keep track of the moving ball and when it is rolled to him he will be able to catch the ball without missing.

Behavioral Activity—To keep track of a moving ball and when it is rolled to him he will be able to catch it.

Success Level—
   (a) Teacher Expectancy—Each child.
   (b) Learner Requirement—Catch the ball without missing.

3.23 Visual Memory

To improve the visual memory of preschool children so that by the end of three months each child will recognize a simple tune and be able to respond by performing without redemonstration and without error a simple circle dance he learned in the early part of the year.

Critique:

Goal—To improve the visual memory of preschool children.

Evaluation—So that by the end of three months each child will recognize a simple tune and be able to respond by performing without redemonstration and without error a simple circle dance learned in the early part of the year.

Behavioral Activity—Will recognize a simple tune and be able to respond by performing without redemonstration and without error a simple circle dance learned in the early part of the year.

Success Level—
   (a) Teacher Expectancy—Each child.
   (b) Learner Requirement—Recognize a simple tune and be able to respond by performing without

redemonstration and without error a simple circle dance learned early in the year.[4]

3.24 Figure-Ground Differentiation

To improve in preschool children the abilities of selecting the dominant figures from surrounding backgrounds so that by the end of the year each child can select correctly the dominate figure in eight out of ten pictures.

Critique:

Goal– To improve in preschool children the abilities of selecting the dominant figures from surrounding backgrounds.

Evaluation– So that by the end of the year each child can select correctly the dominant figure in eight out of ten pictures.

Behavioral Activity– Can select correctly the dominant figure.

Success Level–

(a) Teacher Expectancy–Each child.
(b) Learner Requirement–In eight out of ten pictures.

3.25 Perceptual Consistency

To develop in preschool children the ability to constantly perceive the unique characteristic of several different shapes so that when given a bag

---

[4] The phrase "will recognize a simple tune" is actually a measure of auditory memory, and the goal statement could very easily be extended to include *auditory memory* as an additional learning task. In that case it would read, "To improve the auditory and visual memory of preschool children." From this example it should be obvious that the educator may choose to evaluate two perceptual abilities in one statement.

full of blocks of varying sizes, colors and shapes eighty-five percent of the children will be able to classify by shape all of the square blocks, at least five out of the eight round blocks and at least three of the eight triangular blocks.

Critique:

Goal—To develop in the preschool children the ability to constantly perceive the unique characteristic of several different shapes.

Evaluations—So that when given a bag full of blocks of varying sizes, colors, and shapes eighty-five percent of the children will be able to classify by shape all of the square blocks, at least five out of the eight round blocks, and at least three of the eight triangular blocks.

Behavioral Activity—Be able to classify the blocks by shape.

Success Level—

    (a) Teacher Expectancy—Eighty-five percent of the children.

    (b) Learner Requirement—All of the square blocks, at least five out of eight of the round blocks and at least three of the eight triangular blocks.

3.31 Auditory Acuity

To improve the auditory acuity of first-year orchestra students as determined by each student's ability to differentiate and orally identify without error each instrument when listening to a recording of classical music.

Critique:

Goal—To improve the auditory acuity of first-year orchestra students.

Evaluation—As determined by each student's ability to differentiate and orally identify without error each instrument when listening to a recording of classical music.

Behavioral Activity—To differentiate and orally identify instruments when listening to a recording of classical music.

Success Level—

   (a) Teacher Expectancy—Each student.

   (b) Learner Requirement — Identify without error each instrument.

3.32 *Auditory Tracking*

For preschool children to develop their ability to do auditory tracking so that when given all of the necessary equipment including a ball and bases which make clearly distinguishable noises and enough blindfolds and arm bells for each child, all of the children can play blindman's kickball within the normal peer-group expectancy range as determined by subjective teacher analysis.

Critique:

Goal—For preschool children to develop their ability to do auditory tracking.

Evaluation—So that when given all of the necessary equipment including a ball and bases which make clearly distinguishable noises and enough blindfolds and arm bells for each child, all of the children can play blindman's kickball within the normal peer-group expectancy limits as determined by subjective teacher analysis.

Behavioral Activity—Play blindman's kickball.

Success Level—

   (a) Teacher Expectancy—All students.

   (b) Learner Requirement— Within the normal peer-group expectancy limits as determined by subjective teacher analysis.[5]

3.33 *Auditory Memory*

To improve the *Auditory Memory* of first grade children as determined by ninety percent of the class individually reciting from memory without error any three of the five poems they heard repeatedly during the past two weeks.

Critique:

Goal—To improve the auditory memory of first grade children.

Evaluation—As determined by ninety percent of the class individually reciting from memory without error any three of the five poems they heard repeatedly during the past two weeks.

Behavioral Activity—Individually reciting from memory.

Success Level—

   (a) Teacher Expectancy — Ninety percent of the class.

[5] In this game, sometimes referred to as blindman's baseball, the ball is rolled on the ground toward the sound of homeplate. All players at bat and in the field are blindfolded. The batter or kicker tracks the noise of the ball and then kicks it. He then runs bases the same as in kickball by tracking the noises. The team in the field tries to field the ball and put the players out based upon the noise of the ball, runner, etc.

(b) Learner Requirement – Reciting without error any three of five poems they heard.[6]

3.40 Tactile Discrimination

A. To develop in preschool children enhanced tactile discrimination as measured by each child's ability to differentiate accurately one hundred percent of the time between a penny, a nickel, a dime, and a quarter solely by touch.

Critique:

Goal—To develop in preschool children enhanced tactile discrimination.

Evaluation—As measured by each child's ability to differentiate accurately one hundred percent of the time between a penny, a nickel, a dime, and a quarter solely by touch.

Behavioral Activity—To differentiate between a penny, a nickel, a dime and a quarter solely by touch.

Success Level—

(a) Teacher Expectancy—Each child.

(b) Learner Requirement—Differentiate accurately one hundred percent of the time.

B. To develop in preschool children enhanced tactile discrimination so that when given a bag containing twelve items representing four specific texture categories one hundred percent of the children while blindfolded will group correctly by texture at least ten of the twelve items.

---

[6]This objective requires the student to perform orally from memory poems he heard recited. He had to listen attentively and commit to memory the auditory stimuli, the poems. To test his ability to remember what he has heard, he is requested to respond verbally.

Critique:

Goal—To develop in preschool children enhanced tactile discrimination.

Evaluation—So that when given a bag containing twelve items representing four specific texture categories one hundred percent of the children while blindfolded will group correctly by texture at least ten of the twelve items.

Behavioral Activity—While blindfolded will group items by texture.

Success Level—

    (a) Teacher Expectancy—One hundred percent of the children.

    (b) Learner Requirement—Will group correctly by texture at least ten of the twelve items.

C. To develop in visually handicapped children an enhanced tactile discrimination as measured by each child's ability to orally translate with no more than two errors a selection of three paragraphs written in Braille.

Critique:

Goal—To develop in visually handicapped children an enhanced tactile discrimination.

Evaluation—As measured by each child's ability to orally translate with no more than two errors a selection of three paragraphs written in Braille.

Behavior Activity—Orally translating paragraphs written in Braille.

Success Level—

    (a) Teacher Expectancy—Each child.

    (b) Learner Requirement — No more than two errors.

D. To enhance the development of tactile discrimination of girls in the eighth grade home economics class so that when given ten different samples of fabrics ninety percent of the class will be able to identify by touch and write correctly the names of eight or more of the fabric samples.

Critique:

Goal—To enhance the development of tactile discrimination of girls in the eighth grade home economics class.

Evaluation—So that when given ten different samples of fabrics ninety percent of the class will be able to identify by touch and write correctly the names of eight or more of the fabric samples.

Behavioral Activity—Will identify the fabrics by touch and will write the fabric names.

Success Level—

   (a) Teacher Expectancy – Ninety percent of the class.

   (b) Learner Requirement—Will write correctly the names of eight or more of the fabric samples.

3.50 Coordinated Activities

A. To develop the eye-hand coordination of pre-school children so that when given a piece of paper with a circle, a square and a triangle drawn on it, seventy-five percent of the children can reproduce in recognizable form at least two of the three figures on the sheet of paper with crayon.

Critique:

Goal—To develop the eye-hand coordination of pre-school children.

Evaluation—So that when given a piece of paper with a circle, a square and a triangle drawn on it seventy-five percent of the children can reproduce in recognizable form at least two of the three figures on the sheet of paper with crayon.

Behavioral Activity—Can reproduce in recognizable form the figures on paper with crayon.

Success Levels—

(a) Teacher Expectancy — Seventy-five percent of the children.

(b) Learner Requirement—Can reproduce at least two of the three figures on the sheet of paper.

B. To develop the eye-hand coordination of first grade children as measured by each child's ability to copy in distinguishable form at least ninety percent of the printed upper case letters of the alphabet.

Critique:

Goal—To develop the eye-hand coordination of first grade children.

Evaluation—As measured by each child's ability to copy in distinguishable form at least ninety percent of the printed upper case letters of the alphabet.

Behavioral Activity—Copy printed upper case letters of the alphabet.

Success Level—

(a) Teacher Expectancy—Each child.

(b) Learner Requirement — To copy in distinguishable form at least ninety percent.

C. To develop the eye-hand coordination of first grade children as measured by: (a) each child's ability to successfully catch three out of five times a playground ball which is thrown to him from a distance of approximately ten feet; (b) each child's ability to throw a beanbag up in the air and catch it five times in succession.

Critique:

Goal—To develop the eye-hand coordination of first grade children.

Evaluation—As measured by (a) each child's ability to successfully catch three out of five times a playground ball which is thrown to him from a distance of approximately ten feet; (b) each child's ability to throw a beanbag up in the air and catch it five times in succession.

Behavioral Activity—(a) Catching a playground ball and (b) throwing a beanbag up in the air and catching it.

Success Level—
   (a) Teacher Expectancy—Each child.
   (b) Learner Requirement—(a) Successfully catch three out of five times a playground ball; (b) to catch a beanbag five times in succession.

D. To develop the eye-foot coordination of primary children so that one hundred percent of the children can successfully kick a stationary playground ball five times in succession and eighty percent can successfully kick a moving playground ball three out of five times.

Critique:

Goal—To develop the eye-foot coordination of primary children.

Evaluation—So that one hundred percent of the children can successfully kick a stationary playground ball five times in succession and eighty percent can successfully kick a moving playground ball three out of five times.

Behavioral Activity—Can kick a stationary playground ball and can kick a moving playground ball.

Success Level—

   (a) Teacher Expectancy—One hundred percent of the children can kick a stationary playground ball and eighty percent of the children can kick a moving playground ball.

   (b) Learner Requirement—A stationary playground ball five times in succession and a moving playground ball three out of five times.

E. To develop the eye-foot coordination of beginning modern dance students as measured by the ability of each student to successfully perform with no error in foot pattern a new movement pattern which is demonstrated no more than once across the floor. Each student will be allowed no more than two trials down the floor.

Critique:

Goal—To develop the eye-foot coordination of beginning modern dance students.

Evaluation—As measured by the ability of each student to successfully perform with no error in foot pattern a new movement pattern which is demonstrated no more than once across the floor. Each student will be allowed no more than two trials down the floor.

Behavioral Activity—Perform a new movement pattern.

Success Level—

   (a) Teacher Expectancy—Each student.

   (b) Learner Requirement—Perform with no error in foot pattern.

F. To develop in children the ability to jump rope so that by the end of the year one hundred percent of the children can perform a two-footed single-bounce jump five successive times, and fifty percent of the children can perform five consecutive times the rope jump skill using an alternating foot pattern.

Critique:

Goal—To develop in children the ability to jump rope.

Evaluation—So that by the end of the year one hundred percent of the children can perform a two-footed single-bounce jump five successive times, and fifty percent of the children can perform five consecutive times the rope jump skill using an alternating foot pattern.

Behavioral Activity—To jump rope.

Success Level—

(a) Teacher Expectancy—One hundred percent and fifty percent.

(b) Learner Requirement—Five successive two-footed single-bounce jumps and five consecutive rope jumps using an alternating foot pattern.[7]

4.00 Physical Abilities

Many physical education programs have as a prime concern the development of organic vigor. Discussions of all the subcategories listed in this classification level can be found in the physical educational literature and gen-

---

[7] The jumping movement is categorized as a locomotor movement; the rope turning is a non-locomotor skill; to be able to perform this movement the learner must be able to coordinate successfully the bilateral movement of the two arms. He must be aware of the relationship of the rope to his body in order to get it over his head since he cannot see the rope when it is behind him. He must also possess eye-foot coordination to

eral goal statements written into some programs. If programs profess to have organic vigor (physical fitness) as a major component, this classification level should prove most beneficial.

Logically, then, developing the learner's physical abilities usually becomes the responsibility of the physical education specialist in most of today's schools. This is a major challenge since, in many instances elementary schools have only one full-time physical education specialist or they share a specialist with another school. In spite of this, many secondary schools base their program upon the assumption that learners come to them prepared to move directly into skilled movement behaviors. Therefore, it is of benefit for the educator to organize and prepare his curriculum in behavioral terms, thereby enabling him to follow closely the achievements of his learners. Though this will take a little time in the beginning, he will find that in the long run, his program is better organized, his evaluations of each learner are more objective, and he is able to provide for each learner a more relevant physical abilities program.

How does an educator go about organizing the physical abilities (or physical fitness) component of the program in behavioral terms? The most logical thing would be to first assess the present physical abilities curriculum and organize it into units. Next, any gaps in the curriculum should be remedied. For example, if the curriculum contains units in endurance, strength, and

---

successfully prepare for and jump the rope as it passes in front of and under him. All of these perceptual abilities and fundamental movements must be part of his movement repertoire in order to succeed with the objectives.

flexibility, but completely neglects agility, this last sub-category would be added as a unit within the curriculum of physical abilities. After these preliminary steps, the educator can then further subdivide each unit into its component parts, again filling in any existing gaps. This provides the basic outline for a complete physical abilities program from which an educator can construct a behaviorally stated curriculum.

Perhaps, as a beginning step toward stating the curriculum in behavioral terms, the educator should write goal statements for all the listed units. After selecting the best instruments or performances for measuring the stated unit goals, he can develop his behavioral objective statement. The educator need not restrict his evaluation to one instrument or learner performance; he may use two or more instruments or learner performances or may even combine them to allow for a more comprehensive evaluation of his stated goal. These unit behavioral objectives usually are stated in such a way (with a teacher-expectancy and learner-success criterion) that they can be utilized to evaluate the class as a group. By removing teacher-expectancy, the behavioral objective can be utilized to evaluate an individual learner. Stating the unit of a particular curriculum in behavioral terms, being sure to incorporate comprehensive evaluations for each unit, is a great accomplishment. Behavioral objectives for the specific variables of each unit can now be written.

In some instances, writing behavioral statements for gross units is not adequate because the entire unit needs to be subdivided for purposes of effective evaluation. An excellent example of this is the subcategory or unit component termed strength. In order to measure strength effectively, the muscular strength in each of the particular areas of the body has to be measured. Therefore, the educator would probably begin constructing evaluation statements for each specific variable of the unit termed strength.

Suppose an educator has incorporated in his physical fitness program, activities which are designed to increase overall body strength, he would identify the body areas which he desires the learners to develop. He then writes his intentions for that particular unit in a goal statement. After assessing existing equipment and financial assets and perusing the literature to become knowledgeable about the measurement of strength, he selects those instruments most feasible for measurement in his situation. Once he has made these kinds of decisions, the educator is ready to add the evaluation statements to the goal statement, thus forming a complete behavioral objective statement that measures each specific variable of the unit constructed to meet the needs of his group. More than likely his curriculum will not change, since body parts do not change and methods of developing strength in particular body parts remain constant. Therefore, in order to use this same objective with its multiple evaluation statements the following year, he need only make modifications in success-level criteria and teacher-expectancy if appropriate to meet the needs of any new group of learners.

His behavioral objective for the unit on strength and the corresponding evaluation statements designed to measure one particular variable would be organized in the following fashion:

Unit Objective on Development of Overall Body Strength

To improve the *overall body strength* of *eighth grade boys* so that by the end of the six-weeks unit on strength development *ninety-five percent of the boys* will obtain an *increase in strength measurements for each of the following body areas:*

grip strength as measured by the hand dyno-mometer so that by the end of the unit the learner will demonstrate an increase of five pounds over the pretest measurement.

arm strength as measured by the learner per-forming ten pull-ups more than he could at the beginning of the unit and twenty push-ups more than his pretest measure.

abdominal strength as measured by the learner performing in a period of ten minutes one hun-dred more curl-ups than he could at the begin-ning of the unit.

back strength as measured by the appropriate subtest of the Physical Fitness Index in which the learner shows some increase in score over the pretest measure.

leg strength as measured by the cable tensiome-ter in which the learner increases his score by at least ten pounds for each leg.

It should be recognized that the unit behavioral objective contains each of the components of a well written behavioral objective. In the goal statement, there is an identified learning task (*overall body strength*), an identified learner group (*eighth grade boys*), and an implied domain (physical abilities—*psychomotor*). In the evaluation statement, the reader can identify a stated teacher expectancy (*ninety-five percent of the boys*) and can also identify the learner's required level of success (*increase in strength measurements* for each of the body areas). The evaluation statements for each specific variable included in the unit dealing with the development of overall body strength contains the specific variable and required success level of the learner.

When the educator is organizing his curriculum in behavioral terms and follows the illustrated format, he has a comprehensive evaluation of his entire unit and because of the way his evaluation statements are formed he will be able to identify individual learner weaknesses and perhaps even weak areas in his training program. Being a realistic educator, however, he realizes that all boys will not achieve to the same degree, so he is saying, in essence, in his *unit behavioral objective* that *he will consider this unit on overall body strength development successful if at least ninety-five percent of the learners can reach the stated learner-success levels in the evaluation statements designed to measure one variable.* All units within a physical abilities curriculum could be organized in this fashion thereby giving comprehensive evaluations of the total curriculum in this area.

Following are isolated examples of behavioral objective statements provided for the reader in an effort to facilitate his understanding of the movement behaviors unique to this classification level.

4.00 *Physical Abilities*

Physical abilities have been previously defined as those physical characteristics which when developed to a high degree provide the learner with a *sound, efficiently functioning body*. These physical characteristics include muscular and cardiovascular endurance, overall strength, flexibility and agility.

4.00 Physical Abilities

To improve the overall physical fitness of each intermediate child at Vermont Elementary School so that given one year of physical education and a pre- and post-test of the seven items of the AAHPER Youth Fitness Test Battery, each child will show improved performance by achieving minimum gains of at least:

(1) five pull-ups

(2) twenty-five sit-ups

(3) one-second decrease in time to perform the 40-yard shuttle run.

(4) one-second decrease in time to perform the 50-yard dash

(5) three-seconds decrease in time to perform the 600-yard walk-run

(6) five-foot increase in distance in the softball throw

(7) five-inch increase in performance of the standing broad jump.

4.10 Endurance

Endurance has been defined as the body's ability to supply and use oxygen during strenuous activity. When comparing two learners performing strenuous activity, the more physically fit learner will be obvious because he will be able to *endure* the activity for a longer period of time.

4.11 *Muscular Endurance*

To improve the muscular endurance of eleventh-grade wrestling students as measured by the Rogers Physical Fitness Index, Strength Index, with at least seventy-five percent of the boys scoring in the third quartile or above as compared to the appropriate sex, weight, and age norm group.

Critique:

Goal—To improve the muscular endurance of eleventh-grade wrestling students.

Evaluation—As measured by the Rogers Physical Fitness Index, Strength Index, with at least seventy-five percent of the boys scoring in the third quartile or above as compared to the appropriate sex, weight, age norm group.

Behavioral Activity—Performance on the Rogers Physical Fitness Index, Strength Index.

Success Level—

  (a) Teacher Expectancy—Seventy-five percent of the boys

  (b) Learner Requirements—Scoring in the third quartile or above as compared to the appropriate sex, weight, age norm group.

4.12 *Cardiovascular Endurance*

A. To improve the cardiovascular endurance of seventh-grade boys as measured by a decrease in resting heart rate following a half-mile run for at least ninety percent of the students and a decrease for each student of at least two seconds in time for the 600-yard run.

Critique:

Goal—To improve the cardiovascular endurance of seventh-grade boys.

Evaluation—As measured by a decrease in resting heart rate following a half-mile run for at least ninety percent of the students, and a decrease for each student of at least two seconds in time for the 600-yard run.

Behavioral Activity—A half-mile run and 600-yard run.

Success Level—

  (a) Teacher Expectancy—Ninety percent and each student.
  (b) Learner Requirement—decrease in resting heart rate following a half-mile run and decrease of at least two seconds in time for 600-yard run.

B. To improve the cardiovascular endurance of varsity track runners so that given two weeks of training followed by the Harvard-Step Test, each runner's recovery period pulse count will decrease sufficiently to put the runner into the next highest classification level when compared to the established norms.

Critique:

Goal—To improve the cardiovascular endurance of varsity track runners.

Evaluation—So that given two weeks of training followed by the Harvard-Step Test, each runner's recovery period pulse count will decrease sufficiently to put the runner into the next highest classification level when compared to the established norms.

Behavioral Activity—Performing the Harvard-Step Test.

Success Level—

(a) Teacher Expectancy—Each runner.
(b) Learner Requirement—Recovery period pulse count will decrease sufficiently to put the runner into the next highest classification level when compared to the established norms.

4.20 Strength

Strength, the reader will recall, has been defined as the learner's ability to exert a maximum amount of force against resistance.

A. To improve the grip strength of varsity tennis players so that given a six-week training program followed by a hand dynamometer test, ninety percent of the players will increase their grip strength by at least five pounds above their pretraining measurement.

Critique:

Goal—To improve the grip strength of varsity tennis players.

Evaluation—So that given a six-week training program followed by a hand dynamometer test, ninety percent of the players will increase their grip strength by at least five pounds above their pretraining measurement.

Behavioral Activity—Performance on a hand dynamometer test.

Success Level—

(a) Teacher Expectancy—Ninety percent of the players.
(b) Learner Requirement—Increase their grip

strength by at least five pounds above their pre-training measurement.

B. To improve the arm strength of elementary children as measured by each child's ability to perform at least five pull-ups and at least five push-ups more than he could perform at the beginning of the year.

Critique:

Goal—To improve the arm strength of elementary children.

Evaluation—As measured by each child's ability to perform at least five pull-ups and five push-ups more than he could perform at the beginning of the year.

Behavioral Activity—To perform pull-ups and push-ups.

Success Level—

(a) Teacher Expectancy—Each child.
(b) Learner Requirement—At least five pull-ups and at least five push-ups more than he could perform at the beginning of the year.

4.30 Flexibility

A flexible body is often referred to as a supple body which manifests graceful easy-flowing bending and twisting movement. Limber is another term used when making reference to flexibility. This ability has been defined previously in this text as the range of motion that the learner is capable of achieving in the joints of his body.

4.30 Flexibility

To increase the body suppleness (measured trunk-hip flexibility) of elementary children. By the end of the year eighty percent of the children should be able to bend forward from a standing position and lay the palms of the hands flat on the floor keeping the feet together and legs straight. This position should be held for at least fifteen seconds.

Critique:

Goal—To increase the suppleness (measured trunk-hip flexibility) of elementary children.

Evaluation—By the end of the year eighty percent of the children should be able to bend forward from a standing position and lay the palms of the hands flat on the floor keeping the feet together and legs straight. This position should be held for at least fifteen seconds.

Behavioral Activity—Bend forward from a standing position.

Success Level—

(a) Teacher Expectancy—Eighty percent of the children.

(b) Learner Requirement—Lay the palms of the hands flat on the floor keeping the feet together and legs straight. This position should be held for at least fifteen seconds.

4.40 *Agility*

As the reader will recall, agility is composed of varying abilities of the learner to accomplish rapid movements of the entire body in different directions and in response to unexpected situations. It includes the ability to change direction, make sudden stops and rapid starts, develop a quick reaction time and improve finger dexterity. Activities requiring agility of movement in-

clude games of tag, dodging in football, pivoting in basketball, tumbling in free-exercise, typing, and playing
any type of instrument requiring finger manipulations
such as piano, violin and guitar.

4.40 Agility

To improve the agility of seventh-grade girls as determined by each girl's ability to increase by at least
three the number of squat-thrusts performed during
one minute and to decrease by two seconds the time
to run the 40-yard shuttle run.

Critique:

Goal—To improve the agility of seventh-grade girls.

Evaluation—As determined by each girl's ability to increase by at least three the number of squat-thrusts
performed during one minute and to decrease by two
seconds the time to run the 40-yard shuttle run.

Behavioral Activity—Perform squat-thrusts; run 40-
yard shuttle run.

Success Level—

  (a) Teacher Expectancy—Each girl.

  (b) Learner Requirement—Increase by three the
     number of squat-thrusts performed in one min-
     ute and decrease by two seconds the time to run
     the 40-yard shuttle run.

5.00 Skilled Movements

To be a highly skilled mover the learner must have,
in addition to appropriate control of his basic movement patterns, highly developed perceptual abilities and

adequate development of the physical abilities which are essential for efficient performance of the particular skilled movement. For example, a gymnast performing on the balance beam must have keenly developed kinesthetic discrimination to maintain balance during stationary poses and locomotor movements; she must also be extremely flexible to perform some of the skilled movements and must possess overall body strength. This does not mean that young children cannot begin skilled movements because they may not possess the same degree of strength or kinesthetic awareness that a performer at the advanced skill level possesses.

The explanation of the skill continuum in the previous chapter states that there are four steps of skill proficiency that each learner climbs, and since the elementary school learner can become highly skilled prior to full development of his perceptual and physical abilities, he should be exposed to skilled movements early in life.

Skill has been previously defined in this text as a movement task that requires learning and practice; it is a relatively complex movement performed with a certain degree of efficiency. The basic inherent movement patterns form the foundations upon which the learner builds his skilled movements.

Skilled movements are found in almost every area of the educational curriculum, the most obvious, of course, being the fine arts, vocational programs, and the physical education programs. All sports, dance, recreational, and manipulative skills fall in this classification level.

5.10 Simple Adaptive Skill

A. To improve the ability of high school boys to perform the fifty-yard hurdle run as measured by each boy decreasing his running time by at least one second and knocking down no more than one hurdle.

Critique:

Goal—To improve the ability of high school boys to perform the fifty-yard hurdle run.

Evaluation—As measured by each boy decreasing his running time by at least one second and knocking down no more than one hurdle.

Behavioral Activity—Running the fifty-yard hurdle run.

Success Level—
   (a) Teacher Expectancy—Each boy.
   (b) Learner Requirement—Decreasing running time by at least one second and knocking down no more than one hurdle.

B. To improve the punting skills of high school varsity football players so that when given a skill drill utilizing ground targets placed at varying locations and distances each boy can punt successfully with accuracy and distance, nine out of ten footballs.

Critique:

Goal—To improve the punting skill of high school varsity football players.

Evaluation—So that when given a skill drill utilizing ground targets placed at varying locations and distances each boy can punt successfully with accuracy and distance, nine out of ten footballs.

Behavioral Activity—Punt a football.

Success Level—
- (a) Teacher Expectancy—Each boy.
- (b) Learner Requirement—Can punt successfully with accuracy and distance nine out of ten footballs.

C. To improve the typing skill of first-year typing students as measured by ninety percent of the class typing at least thirty words per minute during a five-minute typing test with no more than five errors.

Critique:

Goal—To improve the typing skill of first-year typing students.

Evaluation—As measured by ninety percent of the class typing at least thirty words per minute during a five-minute typing test with no more than five errors.

Behavioral Activity—Performance on a five-minute typing test.

Success Level—
- (a) Teacher Expectancy—Ninety percent of the class.
- (b) Learner Requirement—Typing at least thirty words per minute with no more than five errors.

5.20 *Compound Adaptive Skill*

A. To improve the catching and batting skills of seventh-grade physical education boys so that when given a softball skill test ninety-five percent of the boys can successfully field a batted grounder three out of five times, can successfully catch a fly ball five out of six times, and can hit, at least in the infield, a pitched ball five out of ten times.

Critique:

Goal—To improve the catching and batting skills of seventh grade physical education boys.

Evaluation—So that when given a softball skill test ninety-five percent of the boys can successfully field a batted grounder three out of five times, can successfully catch a fly ball five out of six times, and can hit at least in the infield a pitched ball five out of ten times.

Behavioral Activity—Can field a batted grounder, can catch a fly ball and can hit a pitched ball.

Success Level—

(a) Teacher Expectancy—Ninety-five percent of the boys.

(b) Learner Requirement—Successfully field a batted grounder three out of five times, successfully catch a fly ball five out of six times, and hit, at least in the infield, a pitched ball five out of ten times.

B. To improve the serving skill of varsity tennis players as measured by each player's ability to correctly serve into the proper receiving court at designated spots 9 out of 10 balls which go no more than 15 inches above the top of the net.

Goal—To improve the serving skill of varsity tennis players.

Evaluation—As measured by each player's ability to correctly serve into the proper receiving court at designated spots 9 out of 10 balls which go no more than 15 inches above the top of the net.

Behavioral Activity—Serving a tennis ball.

Success Level—

(a) Teacher Expectancy—Each player.

(b) Learner Requirement—To correctly serve into the proper receiving court at designated spots 9 out of 10 balls which go no more than 15 inches above the top of the net.

5.30 Complex Adaptive Skills

A. To improve the ability of participants in the advanced gymnastics class to perform a series of one round-off, two back handsprings, one aerial back handspring and one back somersault as measured by each pupil receiving from the judges no lower than a five point rating for his performance of the series.

Goal—To improve the ability of participants in the advanced gymnastics class to perform the series of one round-off, two back handsprings, one aerial back handspring and one back somersault.

Evaluation—As measured by each pupil receiving from the judges no lower than a five point rating for his performance of the series.

Behavioral Activity—Performance of a series of gymnastic stunts.

Success Level—
  (a) Teacher Expectancy—Each pupil.
  (b) Learner Requirement—Receive from the judges no lower than a five point rating for his performance of the series.

6.00 Non-Discursive Communication

The movement behaviors categorized in this classification level include those obvious *movement expressions* which are a part of every learner's movement repertoire and *movement interpretations* which include any efficiently performed skilled movements and movement patterns designed to communicate a message to a viewer.

The educator will not write behavioral objectives for the first subcategory, Expressive Movement, but the reader will argue that any curriculum that utilizes gestures and facial expression such as a drama class would have behavioral statements developed. These kinds of movements, however, would be categorized under creative movement because *they are used to communicate to a viewer*. In reality, they are exaggerated expressive movement behaviors.

Usually, the educator would begin developing behavioral objectives statements at the subcategory of Interpretive Movement. To refresh the reader's memory, aesthetic movement was defined earlier as skilled movement performed with a high degree of efficiency. In other words, the learner is performing at the advanced skill level; creative movements are usually more prevalent in dance choreographies and utilized to provide for a viewer a dynamic image. At the higher levels of creativity, the highly skilled advanced performer is found. At the lower levels of creativity is found the young learner who is involved in movement exploration.

Following are a few behavioral objectives which illustrate the kinds of movement behaviors which fall into this classification level.

6.20 *Interpretive Movement*

A. To develop in preschool children the ability to demonstrate rhythmic creative movement so that, when given the opportunity, at least seventy-five percent of the children will be able to create their own movement sequence and perform it to music. Each child will be judged successful if the performance of his movement sequence lasts at least thirty seconds, if there is a recognizable rhythmic pattern, if he keeps time with the music, and if he utilizes at least two examples of a locomotor movement and one example of non-locomotor movement.

Critique:

Goal—To develop in preschool children the ability to demonstrate rhythmic creative movement.

Evaluation—So that, when given the opportunity, at least seventy-five percent of the children will be able to create their own movement sequence and perform it to music. Each child will be judged successful if his performance of his movement sequence lasts at least thirty seconds, if there is a recognizable rhythmic pattern, if he keeps time with the music and if he utilizes at least two examples of a locomotor movement and one example of a non-locomotor movement.

Behavioral Activity—Be able to create their own movement sequence and perform it to music.

Success Level—

- (a) Teacher Expectancy—Seventy-five percent of the children.
- (b) Learner Requirement—Each child will be judged successful if his performance of his movement sequence lasts at least thirty seconds, if there is a recognizable rhythmic pattern, if he keeps time with the music, and if he utilizes at least two examples of a locomotor movement and one example of a non-locomotor movement.

B. To develop in primary children the abilities to design their own series of movements in free response activities so that by the end of the year each child will be able to create a series of locomotor and non-locomotor movements and perform his choreography for one minute to music. The choreography must contain a minimum of three recognizable locomotor movements and at least four recognizable non-locomotor movements.

Critique:

Goal—To develop in primary children the abilities to design their own series of movements in free response activities.

Evaluation—So that by the end of the year each child will be able to create a series of locomotor and non-locomotor movements and perform his choreography for one minute to music. The choreography must contain a minimum of three recognizable locomotor movements and at least four recognizable non-locomotor movements.

Behavioral Activity—Create locomotor and non-locomotor movements and perform choreography for one minute to music. Choreography must contain at least three recognizable locomotor and four recognizable non-locomotor movements.

Hopefully, the reader is better equipped, after reading the sample behavioral objectives, to begin categorizing movement behaviors relevant to his curriculum and classifying them into one of the levels of this taxonomy in order to construct behavioral objective statements.

CHAPTER V

Review of Literature

A SIMPLIFIED INTRODUCTION
TO THE PHYSIOLOGY OF MOVEMENT

A taxonomy is a framework to be utilized by educators who are concerned with structuring meaningful sequential curricula for their students. It improves professional communication by facilitating the beneficial exchange of ideas. This framework is provided to assist educators in identifying the relevant movement behaviors essential for their particular curriculum. With this foundation, it is easier to recognize and categorize meaningful movement behaviors. Once the essential behaviors have been identified, the next step is to incorporate them into the program plan by making a formal statement of educational intent. In other words, the educator can develop a goal statement which has evolved from the identification of essential behaviors.

The psychomotor domain deals with observable voluntary human movement. These voluntary movements require the use of muscles, nerves, proprioceptors and the central nervous system. Proprioceptors respond like tiny transistors relaying information to the central nervous system regarding position in space of the acting body parts. Through involvement of numerous movement activities these organs develop, becoming more efficient integrated units.

The progressive neuromuscular maturation of the child provides the essential foundation for increased development of psychomotor activities. The movement skills of preschool children are primarily restricted to large muscle coordinations such as running, climbing, pushing and pulling. Through increases in body size, strength, and development of motor skills, the child's perceptual abilities are modified. Perception, being a process of information extraction, continually changes as a function of learning and experiences. In other words, a child will select those portions of his sensory impressions which have value to him.

Perception and motor functions play a vital role in the various stages during the growth and development of the individual. For every sensory activity—reception— there results an accompanying motor reaction— response. As a matter of fact, skeletal muscles contract only if stimulated. Since skeletal muscles usually act in groups, most movements are the products of the coordinated action of several muscles. This coordination of movement effort is controlled by the cerebellum. In addition to coordinating the activities of groups of muscles, the cerebellum assists with the maintenance of equilibrium, control of posture, and it functions below the level of consciousness to make movements smooth, steady and coordinated.[1]

There are three basic kinds of responses, reflexes, maturational (inherent), and acquired (learned). The reflex responses are automatically elicited as a result of stimulation and occur without learning. The matura-

[1] Catherine Parker Anthony, *Textbook of Anatomy and Physiology*, 6th ed. (St. Louis: C. V. Mosby Co., 1963), p. 214.

tional responses are inherent within the organism. Once a child is capable of performing one of the inherent movement patterns, the pattern can be facilitated by experiences or practice. Lack of opportunity to practice has been known to delay the emergence of a maturational response. Both of these types of response are regarded as universal. The third response, acquired, is a complex response resulting from learning.

Obviously, behavior is shaped by the complex interplay of innate abilities, maturation and learning. The psychomotor domain taxonomy is built upon this interplay. The first classification level is dependent upon innate abilities. Level two is primarily built upon maturational response. Levels three and four are chiefly dependent upon both maturation and learning. While levels five and six can be thought of as acquired skills or learned responses.

General Literature

Man is a product of both nature and nurture. The relationship between man's heredity and environment produces the level of biological, psychological and social development which he is capable of achieving. Heredity determines the potential he is capable of attaining in a given environment. The environment supplies him with stimuli which enhance the patterns of response already prepared by maturation. Environment also provides situations conducive to learning new and altering old patterns of behavior.

Movement behaviors evolve during the growth and development of the child. Research has disclosed that movement behaviors develop in a patterned manner during the first year of a child's life. Therefore it is extremely important for the educator to understand that behavior is highly patterned and structured and that much of what the child does actually unfolds rather than being taught. When an educator knows where a child is in his development of movement behaviors, he is better prepared to structure for him movement experiences to facilitate his development. Ames[2] cautions against overteaching the child who is developmentally not ready.

Obviously then, neuromuscular maturation rather than practice is the primary antecedent of locomotor development. According to Mussen, et al.,[3] advanced neural development, increased muscular strength, and change in body proportions are the prerequisites to a child's advancement from one stage of locomotor development to another. Once the child is capable of performing the basic locomotor behaviors, practice enhances coordination and helps the child minimize extraneous interfering movements. They also maintained that attempting to facilitate earlier development of some skills before a child is maturationally ready can be as detrimental as depriving the child of the stimulus entirely.

The basic problem of psychomotor development for each learner is that of adjusting physical activity to his own capabilities and bodily proportions. The learner

---

[2] Louise Bates Ames, "Individuality of Motor Development," *Journal of the American Physical Therapy Association* 46 (February 1966): 121–27.

[3] Paul Henry Mussen, et al., *Child Development and Personality*, 3d ed. (New York: Harper and Row, 1969), p. 178.

is faced with this problem throughout his life. Although hereditary characteristics place a limit on an individual's level of development, his environment will determine the degree to which he will achieve his hereditary potentialities. An individual's behavioral level at any given time in his life is a product of both maturation and learning.

The development of self-concept involves a process of gradual differentiation as the learner begins to distinguish himself from others through his movement activities. With the maturation of sensory mechanisms and of musculature, he begins the process of exploration, thus adding to his affective and his psychomotor development.

Maturation refers to developmental, anatomical, physiological, and chemical changes. These are based upon hereditary characteristics which develop (mature) with the passage of time. It is likened to an unfolding of a predetermined design which is essentially hereditary in origin. These innate sequences and patterns are not influenced by external forces. Loree[4] stated that included in maturation is the fact that the nervous system often anticipates a new function, environment does not create the function. Most behavioral changes are due to an interaction between maturation and learning. Maturation is of importance in determining when a learner is ready to learn a particular task.

Ruch[5] listed three levels to the maturational pro-

---

[4] Ray M. Loree, "Relationships Among Three Domains of Educational Objectives," *Contemporary Issues in Home Economics*, A Conference Report, National Education Association (Washington, D. C., 1965).

[5] Floyd L. Ruch, *Psychology and Life* (Chicago: Scott, Foresman and Co., 1958), pp. 31–63.

cess. The first level is recognized by global, undifferentiated mass activity. The second level is represented by activity which is differentiated with movement being more localized, and the third level is manifested in integrated movement. Though maturation follows the same general sequence, it is not uniform for all children. The differences occur in rate and extent of individual development. Many investigators have verified the fact that no amount of practice will produce behavior patterns until a certain level of maturation is attained.

Gesell[6] stated that during embryogenesis, the formation of the human embryo, muscle function precedes neural, motor nerves are functional before sensory nerves, and the organism is sensitive to proprioceptors, sensory end organs located in muscles and tendon, prior to exteroceptor sensitivity. Motor patterns are laid down in the organism prior to actual experience and utilization. Ontogenetically, all behavior has both a motor origin and aspect. The basic neuromotor equipment for such acts as locomotion, prehension, and perception is developed prior to actual use.

According to Gesell[7] the embryology of behavior can be viewed in terms of posture. The neuromuscular system operating with the skeletal system determines a child's orientation to the physical world. Posture is the position assumed by the whole body or by parts of the body in order to maintain an attitude or execute a movement. Static posture produces an attitude or pos-

[6] Arnold Gesell, *The Embryology of Behavior* (New York: Harper, 1945), pp. 27–31.
[7] Ibid., p. 46.

tural set which presupposes a completed movement or action. Movement or dynamic posture translates postural set into an adaptive movement.

In the human embryo the nerve cells in the central nervous system and the muscle fibers in the human body develop independently. During infancy, connections which are normally common to all individuals develop. Sperry[8] explained that as each nerve develops from the central nervous system, it is guided to its predestined terminal contact point by a chemical environment. It is this chemical affinity which determines the specialized connection of the nerve.

Specific movements which are characteristic of the species, rather than being unique for each individual, are represented within the cortex. Gelhorn[9] reported that by stimulating various points in the motor cortex, definite patterns of movement resulted. It is believed by some that movements rather than muscles are represented in the cortex. Adrian[10] stated that though the mind orders particular movements, the execution of the movement is carried out by the lower levels of the nervous system.

Cooper and Glassow[11] distinguished inherent movement patterns which are characterized by basic

[8] R. W. Sperry, "Mechanism of Neural Maturation," *Handbook of Experimental Psychology*, S. S. Stevens, ed. (New York: John Wiley, 1951), pp. 236–80.

[9] Ernest Gelhorn, *Physiological Foundation of Neurology and Psychiatry* (Minneapolis: University of Minnesota Press, 1953), pp. 50–95.

[10] E. D. Adrian, "The Physiological Basis of Perception," *Brain and Consciousness*, E. Adrian, et al., (Oxford: Blackwell, 1954).

[11] John M. Cooper and Ruth B. Glassow, *Kinesiology* (St. Louis: C. V. Mosby Co., 1963), pp. 163–67.

similarities from reflex responses which do not vary and are performed without conscious intent. The inherent movement patterns of man are not stereotyped; there may be differences in detail but the basic similarities will still exist. These similarities are not learned responses but appear in the human infant without learning; therefore, common patterns of behavior occur without conscious control or awareness. These inherent movements in man have long been considered by educators as fundamental big muscle activity for the ambulant individual.

Though some movement patterns are innate, there still exists the need for learning experiences to enhance the development of movement skills. Improvement in performance of innate movement patterns is accomplished with practice. These patterns appear naturally at various critical stages in a learner's development and should be practiced at this time to facilitate skill development. Some earlier investigations have found that practice interfered with the development of instinctive reflex behavior in chicks. Perhaps the implication here could be that if the learner does not experience practice in these basic patterns at the time the nervous system is ready for them, the patterns will never reach their full potential.

Wild[12] concluded that the development of basic patterns into intricately timed activity, depends on a highly sensitive proprioceptive mechanism. It is the cue

[12]Monica R. Wild, "The Behavior Pattern of Throwing and Some Observations Concerning Its Course," *Research Quarterly*, vol. 9 (1938), pp. 20–24.

from both cutaneous sensations and interoceptors that provide the feedback system essential for skilled movement.

Gardner[13] equated the body's feedback system to that of a computer. The receptors, both cutaneous and interoceptors, initiate such fundamental reflex responses as the flexion reflex, the extensor thrust reflex, and the magnet reflex. Such stimuli detected by sensory receptors inform control centers about the instant of impact and the changing contact with the surface. These feedbacks are essential for timing during abrupt changes in movement sequences and in achieving the needed transitional phases of force and direction which are the basic components of motor learning. Wild[14] suggested that maturational factors are operative when the basic inherent patterns are developing, and after the first six years, learning influences the level of skill an individual attains in a particular inherent pattern.

Gesell[15] calls development an integrative concept which embraces the "total health" of the growing organism. It is manifest in three different types of signs: anatomical, physiological, and behavioral. He stated that though they are all interrelated, the behavior aspect is the most comprehensive index of the maturity and well-being of the learner.

[13] Elizabeth Gardner, "The Neuromuscular Base of Human Movement: Feedback Mechanisms," *Journal of Health, Physical Education and Recreation* (October 1956): 61–62.

[14] Wild, *Throwing*, p. 21.

[15] Arnold Gesell, *Infant Development: The Embryology of Early Behavior* (New York: Harper, 1952).

Developmental Theories

Hebb[16] became concerned with intellectual development after observing the differential effect of early brain damage occurring within the first two years of life and late brain damage occurring after adolescence. He observed an extensive impact on the intellectual development and learning resulting from relative minor brain damage occurring during the first two years of life and the relatively inconsequential effects by comparison of more extensive damage in later life. He also concerned himself with the long period of intellectual immaturity which exists in humans when compared to lower animals.

In his theory he distinguishes two types of brain tissue, the committed tissue and the associative tissue. The committed tissue is tied to sensorimotor functioning; it manages impulses associated with sensory input and motor output, performing only the functions which are chemically inherent within the tissues at birth. The associative tissue presumably must be established by sensorimotor experiences occurring during the first two years of life. This particular type of tissue, according to Hebb, is involved with new learnings.

Hebb theorizes that intellectual development is limited by the ratio of associative tissue to committed tissue—sensorimotor tissue. He concluded that "the larger the proportion of associative tissue to sensorimotor tissue, the greater potential of the organism for

[16] D. O. Hebb, *The Organization of Behavior* (New York: John Wiley and Sons, 1949), pp. 289–94.

complex cognitive development." He contended that the extent of establishment of the associative tissue depended not upon the quality but the quantity of sensorimotor experiences received during the critical period— first two years of life. Thus, according to Hebb, there exist two ways in which individuals can differ in intellectual development—first, the inherited differences in the ratio of associative to committed tissue, and second, the differential extent of sensorimotor experiences during the first two years of life.

The sensorimotor period, the first of four periods in Piaget's[17] theory of developmental milestones which are demarcation points in a child's development, asserts that stimulation of any modality influences or facilitates development in a variety of areas. Piaget suggested that the most crucial period for sensorimotor activity to facilitate perceptual development starts at birth and continues until about the seventh year. He stated that during the first two years of development the amount of stimulation a child receives is more important than the type of stimulation. Thus Piaget and Hebb are in agreement in the belief that quantity of stimulation supersedes quality during the sensorimotor period of life. However, the qualitative aspects of stimulation become essential by at least the age of four. At this age and later, stimulation is most beneficial if it is directly related to the desired behavior one is interested in changing.

In his theory, Piaget postulated four major periods

[17] Jean Piaget, *The Origin of Intelligence in Children* (New York: New York University Press, 1936), pp. 157-268.

of development, the first being the sensorimotor period which occurs prior to the advent of language. He described the major characteristics of this period as sensorimotor intelligence manifesting itself in a series of observable performances. It is during this first period that the child begins the organization of spatial relationships—body image and body position in space.

The second major developmental period in Piaget's theory is termed the period of preoperational thought. It is the beginning of symbolic or semiotic functioning since the child is now capable of representational thought. The inception of operations characterized the third major period in this theory. It is the time of manipulating and conceptualizing about concrete objects. The fourth period is labeled abstract reasoning.

In summary, Piaget's four developmental periods progress from the development of sensorimotor intelligence, to the development of early language and symbolic functions in the preoperational period, to the development of conceptualizations with concrete objects up to the development of abstract reasoning.

Both Hebb and Piaget appear to be suggesting a direct relationship between early meaningful movement experiences and intellectual development.

Terminology

In order to read the literature and comprehend the components of the psychomotor taxonomy, a working vocabulary must be established to insure communicability.

Psychomotor—This is the first term that should be examined. As previously stated, the explanation of the term in Krathwohl's taxonomy emphasized that it is concerned with manipulative skills, motor skills, and acts requiring neuromuscular coordination. Since neuromuscular coordination is the team work or efficiency between nerve impulse and muscle contraction, it cannot logically be considered a major subcategory under the psychomotor domain. Therefore, the term psychomotor distinguishes observable voluntary human movement from involuntary reflex movement.

Perception—Webster defines perception as consciousness or awareness through the medium of the senses. It is the meaning or interpretation placed by the learner upon sensory stimulation.

Perception is the precursor of action; it is the process of becoming aware, attending to, or interpreting stimuli. It involves assembling pertinent cues from various perceptual modalities or stimulus situations. As mentioned previously, the modalities of primary concern to educators are the visual, auditory and kinesthetic—the seeing, the hearing, and the feeling (muscle sense). When the reader sees the terms visual perception, auditory perception, or kinesthetic perception, he must be aware that the term prior to the word perception is simply pinpointing the modality or receptor location of the incoming stimulus. The perceiver interprets the incoming visual, auditory or kinesthetic stimulus in the association area of the brain. This interpretation is based upon his previous learning experiences. Therefore, it can be said that the perceiver categorizes incoming stimuli by giving meaning to them.

Bartley[18] defined perceptual response as the immediate discriminatory response of the learner to his environment. He included all immediate reactions that are initiated from sense organ activation through motor behavior. According to Bartley, then, perception is a process of the learner relating to his environment.

Perception is defined by Kephart[19] as the central portion of the situation-interpretation-action chain, stimulation-perception-response.

In figure 6, the oversimplified diagram shows that a stimulus, in some form, precedes all perception. Since perception is the awareness or interpretation of a stimulus, the preceding statement is logical. A stimulus impinges upon a receptor cell which transduces the imposed energy and activates the afferent nerve impulse traveling to the brain. When the impulse reaches the association area of the brain, interpretation of the stimulus situation occurs. The efferent impulse is activated from the brain and travels down the pathway to the muscle or muscle group which will respond to the interpretation of the stimulus. The muscle or muscle group responds and movement is observed.

Visual perception can be defined as interpretation of stimulation entering the organism by way of the receptor cells of the eye and carried on the afferent pathways to the brain.

[18]S. Howard Bartley, "The Psychology of the Child," *Vision of Children: An Optometric Symposium*, edited by Monroe J. Hirsch and Ralph E. Wick. (Philadelphia: Chilton, 1963), p. 100.

[19]Kephart, *The Slow Learner.*

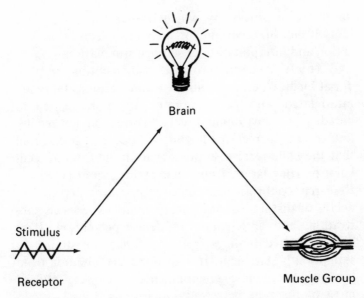

Figure 6—Illustration of Stimulation-Perception-Response Chain

Auditory perception can be defined as interpreta-
tion of stimulation entering the organism by way of the
receptor cells in the hearing organ, the ear, and carried
on the afferent pathways to the brain.

Kinesthetic perception can be defined as an indi-
vidual's interpretation of the relationship of his body to
space. The stimulus is initiated by movement of the
body or body parts and carried on afferent pathways to
the brain. Receptors responsible for kinesthetic perceptions, technically termed propioceptors, are located in
the muscles of the body. Kinesthesis is occasionally referred to as "muscle sense."

For the purposes of this text perception will be

defined as a process by which the learner is aware of himself and his environment. It is the selection, organization and interpretation of sensory stimulation.

The fundamental processes of perception are present at birth. Whether intelligence and learning ability are interrelated with perception, or are more related to heredity and environment, is still something not readily known. For perceptual learning to occur, it is essential that the child receive reinforcement in the form of feedback or stimulation from each of his motor activities. Research confirms that sensory or motor deprivation delays or distorts normal behavior, and experience, motivation, and anticipation influence perception. Denhoff[20] quoted findings from three research studies to support this statement. It was found that children from low socio-economic environments who were hungry most of the time perceived a quarter as being larger in size than did a group of well-fed middle-class children. Children were found to draw larger pictures of Santa Claus ten days prior to Christmas than they did after the holidays. It was also reported that tribes in Africa who live in round houses cannot perceive straight lines as do people in the Western culture who live in angular houses.

It appears from these reported studies that perception depends upon psychological and physiological characteristics of each learner as well as the stimulus situation; it is dependent upon learning and is influenced by

---

[20] Eric Denhoff, "Motor Development as a Function of Perception," *Perceptual-Motor Foundations: A Multidisciplinary Concern*, American Association for Health, Physical Education and Recreation (Washington, D. C., 1969), pp. 49–68.

individual and environmental variables. Cratty[21] calls attention to the fact that an individual's perception is based on past learning experiences which means, the older a child becomes the more experiences he has had, thus, he has more data upon which to base his stimulus interpretations. A learner's perception is also based upon current needs and his individual values and goals.

Since one's perception of a situation depends upon the nature of the learner, it is most important to provide for each learner meaningful experiences to enhance the development of the components so essential to efficient motor responses to presented stimuli.

Cratty divides perception into two major areas, the perception of self and the perception of objects or concepts. Incorporated in the category of perception of self are two subcategories. The first subcategory is defined as the development of an objective body image. This begins during infancy and continues through later life; it is a process of acquiring self-knowledge through visual inspection of surrounding space, and of visual inspection of functioning body parts. The child begins to integrate the kinesthetic sensations of the grasping hand with the visual sensations from the eye movements when following the moving hand reaching for a specific object. The development of a clear body image facilitates the development of a structured self and is basic to continued learning. It is during this development of body image that the learner begins to establish the concept of laterality which is an awareness that two sides of the body exist, and the concept of directionality.

[21] Bryant J. Cratty, *Movement Behavior and Motor Learning* (Philadelphia: Lea and Febiger, 1964), pp. 75–135.

The second subcategory under perception of self deals with body awareness; it assists the learner in gaining additional information about his body in relation to the surrounding space and information about the coordinated activity of body parts.

The second category of Cratty's components of perception deals first with perceptual selection, referred to in the literature as the figure-ground phenomenon. It involves the selection of a dominant object from the ground, or surrounding context. The second subcategory in this area is labeled perceptual speed and deals with the speed with which a judgment or perception about an object or concept is made. The last two subcategories are perceptual flexibility, the ability to imagine variations of a fixed concept of skill, and perceptual structuring. This is a higher level of perceptual skill; it is the structuring, synthesizing and organizing of a task or situation.

Characteristics of Perception—Bruner[22] lists what he considers to be the characteristics of perceptual representation. His first characteristic is listed as the process of comparing the goodness of fit between a model and an object that is being matched to it. This categorical nature of representation is the most unique characteristic of perception. His second characteristic is listed as the summary nature of perception. The things perceived result from preceding and complex integrative

[22] J. S. Bruner, "Neural Mechanisms in Perception," *The Brain and Human Behavior*, vol. 36. Edited by H. C. Solomon, S. Cobb and W. Penfield (Baltimore: Association for Research in Nervous Disorders, 1958).

processes. This is the summating of a multiplicity of excitations into a single effective unit. The last characteristic of perception as listed by Bruner is the autogenetic property of representation. In other words, once representations are established, they generate processes of their own. An example of this is when a student overlearns an activity, he is capable of generating a detailed spatial image of the activity.

Hebb[23] postulated a hierarchy of three levels for perceptual organization. His levels are termed unity, non-sensory figure-ground organization, and identity. Unity is described as the perception of figures separated from the backgrounds. The second level, non-sensory figure-ground organization, is modified by experiences. It is basically a focusing of attention on a particular portion of a stimulus. In Hebb's terms the "boundaries of the figure are not fixed by gradients in the visual field." The last level, identity, represents the associations which are influenced by learning that a child utilizes when interpreting particular familiar stimuli. This is where Hebb's theory of cell assembly plays a major role.

Mechanism of Perception—Cohen[24] lists the physiological mechanisms of perception which are universal for all motor activities as being the eye-vision component, the cervical component, the vestibular component, the body contact component, and the limb posi-

---

[23] Hebb, *The Organization of Behavior*, pp. 19–28.

[24] Leonard A. Cohen, "Mechanisms of Perception: Their Development and Function," *Perceptual-Motor Foundations: A Multidisciplinary Concern*, American Association for Health, Physical Education and Recreation (Washington, D. C., 1969), pp. 23–48.

tion and motion component. These five components make up the physiological perceptual basis of motor activity. Body spatial orientation is the name given to this sensory basis of motor activity. The first, second, and third components can be categorized as postural mechanisms, and components four and five can be categorized as mechanisms responsible for conscious perception of the body's image in relation to its environment.

The first spatial orientation component, eye-vision, helps the individual establish a spatial relationship between himself and the visually fixated object. The learner fixates on an object, interprets various cues from this conformation of the retinal image, and then a spatial perception of distance is made through the stretch-sensitive extraocular muscles of the eye. When both eyes are fixated upon an object, the extraocular muscles which are actually complex sensory organs help the individual to determine the convergence angle. This helps the learner establish the distance of the object enabling him to prepare for reaching or dealing with the object through some motor act.

The second component of spatial orientation is the cervical component located in the neck. This component functions by assisting the individual in relating his head with his trunk and limbs. The angle between the head and the body is perceived through the cervical component helping the individual establish a spatial orientation of the body to the environment—perception of static posture.

The vestibular component, which is the third component of spatial orientation is located in the mastoid bone behind each ear and is composed of two major structures, the semicircular canals and the otolith structures. The semicircular canals function as detectors of any angular or rotary acceleration of the head and the whole body. The inertia of the fluid in these canals causes a pressure on the sensory receptors located in this area thus initiating a nerve impulse. The otoliths, according to Cohen, are sensitive only to gravity.

These postural mechanisms of the visual component help the individual to determine the relationship of his body to the viewed object, and to determine the distance of the object from him. These determinations are essential to efficient functioning in both manipulative and motor skills.

The postural mechanisms of the cervical and vestibular components help the individual to establish body orientation in space by notifying him of acceleration or deceleration to which his body is being subjected, and by providing directional information through these receptors. They provide essential data to the learner for making adjustments in both static and dynamic postures.

The second category, encompassing the last two components of spatial orientation, is that of mechanisms responsible for body image in space. This category includes the body contact component and the limb position and motion component.

The body contact component is significant in spatial orientation of the total body because the contact receptors located in the cutaneous tissue and gluteal muscles are activated when the body is supported in a seated position. In the soles of the feet, the sensory receptors are activated while in a standing position. Both of these areas of body contact relay essential sensory information to add to the learner's perception of himself in his environment.

The limb position and motion component of body spatial orientation, also categorized as an important mechanism to help the individual relate his body image to his environment, have the pertinent receptors located in the articular capsules in all joints. These sensory organs are called joint proprioceptors and function in helping the learner judge the angle of the limb or position of the limb in space. They function cooperatively with tendon receptors and muscle receptors which respond to stretch.

Thus, with the addition of the last two components of spatial orientation, the individual is able to determine the various limb and body positions assumed in space during movement patterns. This type of kinesthetic feedback is essential for the development of high levels of skilled movements. These components of body spatial orientations are essential for the learner's orientation ability and efficient functioning of the whole body or body appendages, while reaching for or locomoting toward a visually fixated object.

Perceptual-Motor—This term implies the interpretation and response an individual makes to a stimulus. Almost everything a person involves himself in must be classified as perceptual-motor. It provides a distinction between voluntary and involuntary responses. Often in the literature, the term perceptual-motor development is found. This actually refers to developmental milestones which are generally assumed to occur in a regular sequence. These defined patterns of growth in children have been verified by studies of Gesell[25] and McGraw.[26] The child is first observed to pass through a phase of random exploratory movements with little or no cortical control. As the child develops, his movements become more purposeful and controlled. The development of controlled movement is sequential, proceeding from the neck to the trunk and the upper extremities to the lower extremities. The large muscle movements develop prior to the precise movements of the small muscles. To recapitulate, the learner progresses from simple to complex movement patterns building upon the innate movement patterns within the individual at birth. These movement experiences form the foundations of the perceptual-motor development.

Many programs for developing perceptual abilities have as their primary goals the development of sensory acuity and motor skills. Recently, there have been research studies that have supported the theory that a wealth of sensory experiences is essential for optimum integrated functioning of the brain. The basic ingredients of most perceptual-motor programs could well be listed as the following: (1) the enhancement of the learner's perception of a body image—the relationship of the body to the surrounding space and an awareness of direction, (2) the development of a sense of dynamic balance, (3) the improvement of basic body movements

[25] Arnold Gesell, *Infant Development*.
[26] Myrle B. McGraw, *The Neuromuscular Maturation of the Human Infant* (New York: Columbia University Press, 1943).

—locomotor and non-locomotor skills, utilizing sym-
metrical and asymmetrical activities to strengthen the
concepts of laterality and bilaterality, (4) the development of specific coordinated movements which include
eye-hand and eye-foot coordinations, (5) the development of manipulative skills, (6) the development of
form perception, and (7) the enhancement of each
learner's natural rhythmic patterns. The visual, auditory
and kinesthetic sensory modalities are all utilized when
attempting to guide a learner through the optimal development of his perceptual abilities.

Delacato[27] bases his perceptual-motor development
theory upon the inherent neurological development of
the individual. He explains neurological organization as
a sequential continuum which forms the basis of human
perceptual abilities. It is a developmental process that
each child should progress through, beginning at birth
and being fairly complete at six years of age. He divides
neurological organization into four significant developmental stages which each child must pass through. When
a child reaches each particular stage, he must be allowed
to master the functional neurological activities prior to
proceeding to the next stage or level. These four stages
are named by the level of neurological functioning. The
first level, which begins around three to twenty weeks of
age, is categorized as neurological functioning at the
level of the pons. The pons is part of the hindbrain and
is located just below the midbrain. Located in the pons
are transverse fibers connected to the cerebellum, which
is the primary organ for motor coordination. The in-

[27]Carl Delacato, *The Diagnosis and Treatment of Speech and
Reading Problems* (Springfield, Ill.: Thomas, 1963).

fant's behavior during this period is characterized as a mobility pattern which is homolateral in nature. Homolaterality of movement is basically a one-sided level of functioning. In other words, a child moves forward by utilizing the arm and leg on the same side of the body extended, while the arm and leg on the opposite side of the body are flexed with head turned toward the flexed limbs.

Beginning around the age of seven to nine months, the level of neurological functioning is at the midbrain. This brain area is located just below the cerebral hemispheres, and is primarily a passage way for sensory and motor tracts and a bridge for higher and lower parts of the nervous system. The child now moves as a bilateral being utilizing opposite appendages for propulsion; the right arm and left leg are used together. Creeping is an excellent example of bilateral movement performed during this stage. This bilateral propulsion is termed cross-patterning by Delacato. At this point in life, the child should begin developing a basis for the concepts of laterality and directionality.

According to Delacato, the child reaches the cortical level of neurological functioning around the age of one year. McGraw also lists cortical control beginning around the first full year of life. Movement is now controlled by the higher centers. The child has progressed from one-sided movement patterns, to two-sided movement patterns, to smooth coordinated cross-patterning.

The last level of development encompasses the stage of cortical hemispheric dominance. The development of hemispheric dominance is the unique characteristic, in neurological terms, that enables man to develop a symbolic language. According to Delacato, this continuum of neurological organization forms the basis of human perceptual abilities.

Delacato's theory, at present, has not been wholly supported by research currently being conducted in laboratories studying brain function. Many neurologists are hesitant to back his work.[28]

Expansion of the movement skills repertoire depends upon neuro-muscular development. According to Gesell,[29] persisting traces of infantile behavior have almost disappeared at about age three. The child is observed to run with greater smoothness, accelerates with more ease, turns sharper corners and performs sudden stops with fewer mishaps. He can jump down from a bottom step with both feet together or with one foot leading slightly.

Several studies involving preschool children have concluded that though neurological maturation is essential, learning does influence the development of such motor skills as talking, writing, buttoning clothes, and lacing shoes. These particular types of skills do not develop unless training or opportunity for imitation is provided.

The child's motor development at the preschool age cannot be isolated from his psychological development since he is constantly relating himself to people around him. Progressive maturation of his neuromuscular system forms the basis for increased movement skill

[28] Bryant J. Cratty, *Perceptual and Motor Development in Infants and Children* (New York: Macmillan, 1970), pp. 253–56.

[29] Arnold Gesell, *The First Five Years of Life*.

development. Learning plays an increasing role in these improvements.

Denhoff[30] states that the motor basis for perceptual development are posture, directionality, laterality and awareness of position of the body in space. He also proclaims the inseparability of motor bases, perception and intelligence when viewing the child and his adjustment to school.

Bowers'[31] program is based upon the recognized sequential patterns of development. In each of the four activity areas, the learner progresses in a sequential order from simple to complex movements, from gross to finely coordinated movements, movements of the neck, the trunk, the upper and then the lower extremities, performance of bilateral movements and then movements depicting the dominant or preferred sides. The program categorizes movement into the following four activity areas: (1) exploratory movements, (2) balance, (3) airborne activities, and (4) hand-eye manipulative skills.

Kephart's[32] program for slow learners is based upon the premise that cognitive development is dependent upon the orderly development of motor patterns. Barsch[33] also believes movement efficiency promotes cognitive development. They both utilize a body organization approach which stresses the development of essential concepts of posture, laterality, directionality,

[30] Denhoff, *Perceptual-Motor Foundations.*
[31] Louis Bowers, *Developmental Activities.*
[32] Kephart, *The Slow Learner.*
[33] Barsch, *Perceptual-Motor Efficiency.*

and awareness of body in space. Doman and Delacato have also built their program upon sequential development of movement patterns stressing the concepts of homologous and cross-pattern movements—concept of laterality and establishment of dominance.

What most of the perceptual-motor programs are saying, in essence, is that structured movement experiences improve perceptual abilities and perhaps facilitate cognitive development. The more successful movement experiences a child is exposed to, the more aware he becomes of his body position in space and his body image in relation to the environment; thus he becomes better able to make necessary bodily adjustment based upon his interpretation of the environment. The more movement experiences he has, the more aware he becomes of the concept of laterality; he is better able to utilize and understand the functions or types of movement he can achieve with both sides of his body and his appendages. The concept of directionality is really the cognitive ability to interpret the meaning of directional words.

Perceptual Abilities—Usually a child with a perceptual handicap is having difficulties with the development of one or more of the perceptual abilities and his interpretation of a stimulus situation does not match the actual situation. Perceptual abilities are essential to efficient functioning in all three of the learning domains. Many of the perceptual-motor programs implemented in the schools today provide children with activities designed to enhance the development of these essential abilities. Most programs are based upon the theory that improved perceptual abilities attained through motor activities will eventually lead to improved academic performance.

Logically then, the next question that should come to the mind of the reader is: If perceptual-motor development programs are based upon activities which facilitate the development of perceptual abilities which are essential for academic achievement, what are these perceptual abilities?

Some of the perceptual abilities which are of prime concern in most of the developmental programs can be categorized, for ease of discussion, by the reception location. These perceptual abilities fall into the visual, auditory, and kinesthetic categories. All are essential, and therefore are not presented here in order of priority. The reader, however, should remain cognizant of the fact that the child is an integrated being who is normally bombarded with incoming stimuli from all of these modalities.

Kinesthesis is often termed "muscle sense." It is the feel that goes along with any movement task or movement pattern; it is an awareness of the moving body or body parts. In perceptual motor programs, teachers provide experiences which assist each learner in the development of *body awareness*. This is the ability to recognize and control the body and its appendages. *Body awareness then becomes in part a function of kinesthesis.* Any program that aims at the strengthening of concepts of *body awareness would incorporate activities to facilitate the learner's concepts of laterality, bilaterality, and dominance.* Also incorporated in most units on body awareness is the concept of directionality; this is the relationship of the learner to the outside world; he masters, hopefully, such concepts as right-left, up-down, front-back. When moving upon command to demonstrate he has mastered the concept of directionality, the learner is, in fact, demonstrating his knowledge of the verbal language which could easily place this particular concept in the cognitive domain.

Body image is also a component of kinesthesis. Scagliotta[34] defines body image as an awareness a learner has about himself which helps him differentiate between himself, others, and the physical world. According to Scagliotta, difficulties with the concept of body-images are indicative of a state of general immaturity.

The *perceptual abilities concerned with visual discrimination* are listed as visual acuity, visual tracking, visual memory, figure-ground discrimination, and perceptual constancy. *Visual acuity is the ability to receive and differentiate between various sights. Visual tracking is the ability to follow with coordinated eye movements symbols and objects.* When an observer is engrossed in a ping pong game and follows with his eyes the flight of the ball, he is practicing visual tracking. *Visual memory is the ability to recall and state verbally or recall and reproduce through writing or drawing some past visual experiences. Figure-ground discrimination is the ability to select the dominant figure from the surrounding background. Perceptual constancy is the ability of the learner to recognize familiar symbols even when they are presented in a different manner or size.*

[34]Edward G. Scagliotta, *Initial Learning Assessment* (San Rafael, Calif.: Academic Therapy Publication, 1970), p. 31.

The *perceptual abilities concerned with auditory discrimination* are listed as auditory acuity, auditory tracking, and auditory memory. *Auditory acuity is the ability to receive and differentiate between sounds and the corresponding pitch and intensity.* In music classes, learners are exposed to intensive training in the area of auditory acuity; often they must differentiate between types of instruments while listening to a recording. Auditory acuity is also of prime concern when teaching a child phonics. *Auditory tracking is the ability to locate sounds and follow their movements. Auditory memory is the ability to recognize and reproduce past auditory experiences.* Asking a child to recall from memory and say the vowel sounds is an example of auditory memory. Requesting a music student to play from memory a certain selection on his trumpet is also an example of auditory memory.

The perceptual-motor development programs also are concerned with the development of *visual-motor coordination*, and therefore, activities are provided which enhance the development of *eye-hand and eye-foot coordinated movement patterns*. Hitting a tennis ball and kicking a moving soccer ball are good examples of eye-hand and eye-foot coordination.

The following terminology is useful to a comprehension of the behaviors which are categorized in the psychomotor domain.

Laterality is the learner's internal awareness of the right and left side of his body. Actually, this is not an acquired concept, but in action programs designed for the development of sensory acuities and motor skills, the learner is exposed to a wealth of stimuli which heighten this awareness. He utilizes both sides of his body in many types of activities, and therefore develops movement efficiency and increases his movement vocabulary.

Directionality is the relationship of the learner's body to the outside world in terms of distances and directions. The spatial perceptions of directionality are learned rather than dependent upon innate neurological functioning. As has been mentioned previously, directionality could really be categorized as one of the lower levels of the cognitive domain.

Dominance refers to the side of the body which takes the lead in a particular activity. The dominant hemisphere of the brain is opposite to the dominant side of the body. This is the same concept referred to as "handedness" or "preferred hand."

Balance is the maintenance of a particular body position. There are two distinct types of balance that are of prime concern to all individuals throughout most of their daily activities, static and dynamic balance. *Static balance is the maintenance of a particular stationary body posture* while *dynamic balance is the maintenance of a stable posture while performing a movement skill.*

Summary

Psychomotor connotes that the mind is involved in a particular movement, therefore, the movement must be a voluntary purposeful movement. Perceptual-motor connotes interpretation of a stimulus and a corresponding response. Once again the mind is involved, therefore the movement must be voluntary. Psychomotor and perceptual-motor appear to be synonymous.

Perception is the process by which a learner becomes aware of himself and his environment through various sense modalities. Visual perception is a learner's interpretation of a stimulus received through the sense organs of sight. Auditory perception is a learner's interpretation of a stimulus received through the sense organs of hearing. Kinesthetic perception is the learner's interpretation of a stimulus received through the organs in muscle. An individual's perception is modified by psychological and physiological characteristics and past learning experiences and is based upon current needs of the learner and his individual values and goals.

Perceptual-motor development programs are based upon sequential patterns of growth and development in children. A child moves through a phase of random exploratory movements to more purposeful controlled movements.

Some of the perceptual abilities identified in various perceptual-motor programs are: (1) the enhancement of kinesthesis which includes the development of a body image and the awareness of the body to the surrounding environment; this incorporates the enhancement of the concepts of laterality and directionality, (2) the development of eye-hand and eye-foot coordinations; (3) the development of visual discrimination which encompasses visual acuity, visual tracking, visual memory, figure-ground discrimination and perceptual constancy, and (4) the development of auditory discrimination which encompasses auditory acuity, auditory tracking and auditory memory.

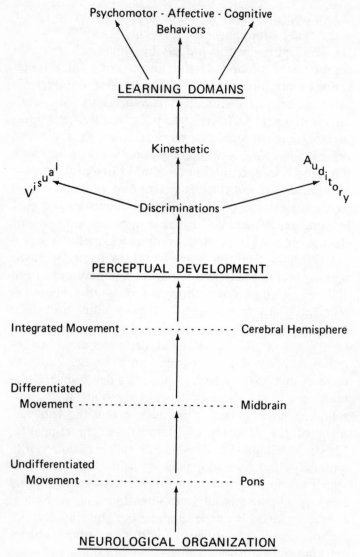

Figure 7—Interrelationships of Neurological Organization, Perceptual
Abilities, and Learning Domains

The development of all of these perceptual abilities is essential for optimal development of the learner's potentials in the cognitive, psychomotor and affective learning domains.

Figure 7 depicts the relationships of the major concepts covered in this chapter. Starting with the neurological organization which is a maturational process inherent within each learner, the characteristic movement patterns appearing at each level of brain functioning can be seen. Of course, the reader must realize that these are not in reality exclusive categories because movement behaviors overlap. Once the learner begins functioning at the level of the cerebral hemispheres, the perceptual abilities have a stable foundation upon which to continually develop for further optimal functioning. The reader should note, even though the chart does not depict it, that the components of the perceptual abilities category actually begin maturing while the learner is progressing through the first developmental sequence. Through meaningful experience the learner improves his perceptual abilities which in turn facilitates his development in the psychomotor, cognitive, and affective domains.

Bibliography

Abernathy, Ruth, and Waltz, Maryann, "Art and Science of Human Movement." *Quest II: Art and Science of Human Movement*. The National Association for Physical Education of College Women and The National College Physical Education Association for Men (April 1964), pp. 1-7.

Adrian, E. D. "The Physiological Basis of Perception." *Brain and Consciousness*. Edited by E. Adrian, et al. Oxford: Blackwell, 1954.

Ames, Louise Bates. "Individuality of Motor Development." *Journal of the American Physical Therapy Association*, vol. 46 (February 1966), pp. 121–27.

Anthony, Catherine Parker. *Textbook of Anatomy and Physiology*, 6th ed. St. Louis: C. V. Mosby Co., 1963, p. 214.

Barsch, Ray H. *Achieving Perceptual-Motor Efficiency: A Space-Oriented Approach to Learning*. Seattle: Seattle Sequin School, 1967.

Bartley, Howard S. "The Psychology of the Child." *Vision of Children*. Philadelphia: Chilton, 1963.

Bayley, N. *Mental and Motor Development Scales*. New York: Psychological Corp., 1969.

Bloom, Benjamin S., ed. *Taxonomy of Educational Objectives Handbook I: Cognitive Domain*. New York: David McKay Co., 1956.

Bowers, Louis. *A Program of Motor Developmental Activities*. Mimeograph ed. Tampa, Florida: University of South Florida, 1961.

Broer, Marion. *Efficiency of Human Movement*. Philadelphia: W. B. Saunders Co., 1960.

Bruner, J. S. "Neural Mechanisms in Perception." Edited by H. C. Solomon, S. Cobb, and W. Penfield. *The Brain and Human Behavior*, vol. 36. Baltimore: Association for Research in Nervous Disorders, 1958.

Bucher, Charles A. *Foundations of Physical Education*. St. Louis: C. V. Mosby Co., 1964.

Cohen, Leonard A. "Mechanisms of Perception: Their Development and Function." *Perceptual-Motor Foundations: A Multi-disciplinary Concern*. Washington, D.C.: American Association for Health, Physical Education, and Recreation, 1969.

Cooper, John M., and Glassow, Ruth B. *Kinesiology*. St. Louis: C. V. Mosby Co., 1963.

Cowell, Charles C., and Wellman, Frances L. *Philosophy and Principles of Physical Education*. Englewood Cliffs, N. J.: Prentice-Hall, 1965.

Cratty, Bryant J. *Movement Behavior and Motor Learning.* Philadelphia: Lea and Febiger, 1964.

_____, *Developmental Sequences of Perceptual-Motor Tasks: Movement Activities for Neurologically Handicapped and Retarded Children and Youth.* Long Island, New York: Educational Activities, 1967.

_____, *Perceptual and Motor Development in Infants and Children.* New York: Macmillan, 1970.

Cruickshank, William M., Bentzen, Frances A., Ratzeburg, Fredrick H., and Tannhauser, Miriam T. *A Teaching Method for Brain-Damaged and Hyperactive Children*. Syracuse: Syracuse University Press, 1961.

Delacato, Carl. *The Diagnosis and Treatment of Speech and Reading Problems*. Springfield, Ill.: Charles C. Thomas, 1963.

Denhoff, Eric. "Motor Development as a Function of Perception." *Perceptual-Motor Foundations: A Multi-disciplinary Concern*. Washington, D. C. American Association for Health, Physical Education and Recreation, 1969.

Ellfeldt, Lois, and Metheny, Eleanor. "Movement and Meaning: Development of a General Theory." *Research Quarterly*, vol. 29 (1958), pp. 264–73.

Gardner, Elizabeth. "The Neuromuscular Base of Human Movement: Feedback Mechanisms." *Journal of Health, Physical Education and Recreation*. (October 1956), pp. 61–62.

Gelhorn, Ernest. *Physiological Foundation of Neurology and Psychiatry*. Minneapolis: University of Minnesota Press, 1953.

Gesell, A., Halverson, H. M., Thompson, H., Ilg, F. L., Castner, B. M., Ames, L. B., and Amatruda, C. S. *The First Five Years of Life: A Guide to the Pre-School Child*. New York: Harper, 1940.

Gesell, Arnold. *The Embryology of Behavior*. New York: Harper, 1945.

────── , "The Ontogenesis of Infant Behavior." Edited by Leonard Carmichael. *Manual of Child Psychology*. New York: John Wiley and Sons, 1946, pp. 295-331.

────── , *Infant Development: The Embryology of Early Behavior*. New York: Harper, 1952.

Hartson, L. D. "Contrasting Approaches to the Analysis of Skilled Movement." *Journal of General Psychology*, vol. 20 (1939), pp. 280-82.

Hebb, D. O. *The Organization of Behavior*. New York: John Wiley and Sons, 1949.

Hirsch, Monroe J., and Wick, Ralph E., eds. *Vision of Children: An Optometric Symposium*. Philadelphia: Chilton, 1963.

Hunt, Valerie. "Movement Behavior: A Model for Action." *Quest II: The Art and Science of Human Movement*. The National Association for Physical Education of College Women and The National College Physical Education Association for Men (April 1964), pp. 57-66.

Jokl, Ernest. "The Acquisition of Skill." *Quest VI: A Symposium on Motor Learning*. The National Association for Physical Education of College Women and the National College Physical Education Association for Men, May 1966.

Kephart, N. E. *The Slow Learner in the Classroom*. Columbus, Ohio: Charles E. Merrill, 1960.

Kibler, Robert J., Barker, Larry L., and Miles, David T. *Behavioral Objectives and Instruction*. Boston: Allyn & Bacon, 1970.

Krathwohl, David R., Bloom, Benjamin S., and Masia, Bertram B. *Taxonomy of Educational Objectives Handbook II: Affective Domain*. New York: David McKay Co., 1964.

✓ Kraus, Hans, and Roab, Wilhelm. *Hypokinetic Disease*. Springfield, Ill.: Charles C. Thomas, 1961.

Laban, R., and Lawrence, F. C. *Effort*. London: McDonald and Evans, 1947.

Langer, Susanne K. *Problems of Art.* New York: Charles Scribner's Sons, 1947.

Loree, Ray M. "Relationships Among Three Domains of Educational Objectives," in *Contemporary Issues in Home Economics.* A Conference Report, National Education Association. Washington, D. C., 1965.

Matthews, Donald K., and Fox, Edward L. *The Physiological Bases of Physical Education and Athletics.* Philadelphia: W. B. Saunders, 1971.

McAshan, H. H. *Writing Behavioral Objectives: A New Approach.* New York: Harper and Row, 1970.

McGraw, Myrle B. *The Neuromuscular Maturation of the Human Infant,* New York: Columbia University Press, 1943.

Metheny, Eleanor. "Movement, Meaning, and the Conative Domain." *Connotations of Movement in Sport and Dance.* Dubuque, Iowa: William C. Brown, 1965, pp. 23-34.

Mohr, Dorothy R. "The Contributions of Physical Activity to Skill Learning," *American Association for Health, Physical Education, and Recreation Research Quarterly,* vol. 31 (1960).

Morehouse, Laurence E., and Miller, Augustus T. *Physiology of Exercise.* St. Louis: C. V. Mosby Co., 1963.

Morgan, Clifford T. "Motor Functions," *Physiological Psychology.* New York: McGraw-Hill, 1965.

Munn, N. L. *Psychology.* Boston: Houghton Mifflin, 1946.

Mussen, Paul Henry, Conger, John Janeway, Kagan, Jerome. *Child Development and Personality,* 3d ed. New York: Harper and Row, 1969.

Movement Group Report. *Workshop Report: Purposeful Action.* Washington, D. C.: The National Association for Physical Education of College Women, 1956.

Piaget, Jean. *The Origin of Intelligence in Children.* New York: New York University Press, 1936.

———, *The Mechanisms of Perception.* Translated by G. N. Seagrim. New York: Basic Books, 1969.

Ragsdale, C. E. "How Children Learn Motor Types of Activities." *Learning and Instruction*. Forty-ninth Yearbook of the National Society for the Study of Education, 1950, pp. 69-91.

Roach, Eugene, and Kephart, Newell. *The Purdue Perceptual-Motor Survey*. Columbus, Ohio: Charles E. Merrill, 1966.

Ruch, Floyd. *Psychology and Life*. Chicago: Scott, Foresman, 1958.

Sachs, Curt. *World History of the Dance*. New York: Bonanza Books, 1937.

Scagliotta, Edward G. *Initial Learning Assessment*. San Rafael, Calif.: Academic Therapy Publications, 1970.

Scott, Gladys M. *Analysis of Human Motion*. New York: Appleton-Century-Crofts, 1963.

Seashore, R. "An Experimental and Theoretical Analysis of Five Motor Skills." *American Journal of Psychology*, vol. 53 (1940).

Simpson, Elizabeth Jane. *The Classification of Educational Objectives: Psychomotor Domain*. University of Illinois, Research Project No. OE 5-85-104, 1966.

Singer, Robert N. *Motor Learning and Human Performance: An Application to Physical Education Skills*. New York: Macmillan, 1968.

Smith, K. U., and Smith, W. H. *Perception and Motor*. Philadelphia: W. B. Saunders, 1962.

Sperry, R. W. "Mechanism of Neural Maturation," *Handbook of Experimental Psychology*. Edited by S. S. Stevens. New York: John Wiley & Sons, 1951, pp. 236-80.

Stone, H. *Applied Anatomy and Kinesiology*. Philadelphia: Lea and Febiger, 1953.

Weymouth, Frank W. "Visual Acuity of Children." *Vision of Children: An Optometric Symposium*. Edited by Monroe J. Hirsch and Ralph E. Wick. Philadelphia: Chilton, 1963.

Wild, Monica R. "The Behavior Pattern of Throwing and Some Observations Concerning Its Course." *Research Quarterly*, vol. 9 (1938), pp. 20-24.